MESILAH

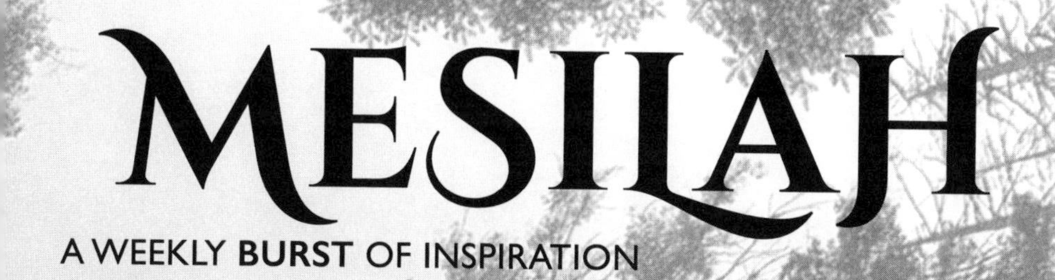

MESILAH

A WEEKLY **BURST** OF INSPIRATION

Aryeh Berzansky

MOSAICA PRESS

Mosaica Press, Inc.

Typeset by Rayzel Broyde

ISBN 13: 978-1-937887-40-7 ISBN-10: 1937887405

Published and distributed by:

Mosaica Press, Inc.

www.mosaicapress.com

info@mosaicapress.com

הסכמת מורי ורבי הגאון רבי יעקב אליעזר שוורצמן שליט"א
ראש ישיבת לייקווד באר"י

Yaakov E. Schwartzman
BETH MEDRASH GOVOHA OF ERETZ YISROEL - LAKEWOOD
Rabbi Aharon Kotler
Institute for Advanced Learning
Jerusalem

יעקב אליעזר שוורצמן
בית מדרש גבוה בא"י - לייקווד
בית מדרשו של רבינו הגדול
מרן הגאון ר' אהרן קוטלר זצוקללה"ה
עיה"ק ירושלים תובב"א

בס"ד, יום ד' לס' ברכה כ"ד מנחם אב תשע"ד

נעים לי מאד להכיר ולהוקיר את ידידי היקר ומאד נעלה, אהוב למעלה ונחמד למטה, שייף עייל ושייף נפיק גריס באורייתא תדירא ולא מחזיק טיבותא לנפשי', המצויין בתוי"ש טהורה ובכל מדה נכונה וישרה, ה"ה הרב ר' אריה ברזנסקי שליט"א, מוותיקי תלמידי ישיבתנו הק' זה רבות בשנים, אשר עלה ונתעלה בין כתליה לאילנא רברבא, וזכה להשפיע הרבה ברוחו הכבירה ונפשו הטהורה על לומדי ישיבתנו הק' בתורה ויר"ש, הן בהבנת הסוגיות והן בהתעוררות לבם וחשקם לתורה, וזכה והצליח לקרבם ולמשכם בעבותות אהבה, לפתוח עיניהם ולהאהיב תורתם ולימודם עליהם, ולהעמידם בקרן אורה בעמל התורה ועבודת השי"ת והמדות ברוב הצלחה וסייעתא דשמיא.

וכעת כאשר אוותה נפשו לזכות את הרבים בפרי רוחו אשר הגה זה שנים בעניני פרשת השבוע ובמוסריה ולימודיה היוצאים ממנה, ומהם דברים אשר היה שולחם מידי שבוע לכמה מתומכי הישיבה הק', והכל לפי סגנונו המיוחד ברעיון קל בהוספת סיפור ומשל מן החיים המושך את הלב בשפה קולחת ונוחה למען יוכל כ"א להבינו ולהשכיל לפום שיעורא דילי', ולהפיק ממנו את התועלת הנרצה.

ומהמעט אשר ראיתי כעת ובעבר, נראה שיש בזה תועלת רבה הן לתלמידי הישיבות הק' בראשית דרכם, והן לבעלי בתים הרוצים להתחזק יותר בעבודתם הרוחנית ועדיין אינם מכירים כ"כ את לשון הקודש ואינם יכולים להפיק תועלת מספרי המוסר והמחשבה המקובלים בישראל, ומן הטעם הזה ומרוב חיבתי להמחבר הדגול יצאתי הפעם חוץ מגדרי לכתוב הסכמה על ספר שלא נכתב בלשון הקודש, דבר שלא הורגלנו בכך בעבר מכמה טעמים, והוא צורך השעה, וגם ניכר שכוונתו לש"ש במידה רבה.

ובזה ברכתי שלוחה לידידי הדגול, שהשי"ת יזכהו להמשיך בדרכו להתעלות בתורה ויר"ש ולהשפיע מאורו על לומדי תורה ומבקשי השי"ת החפצים להתעלות ולהתקרב, מתוך מנוחת הנפש והרחבת הדעת עד כי יבא שלה בב"א.

כעתירת המברך מקרב לב הכו"ח למען תועלת הרבים ולכבוד המחבר הדגול

יעקב אליעזר שוורצמן

Rabbi Yitzchak Berkovits
Sanhedria HaMurchevet 113/27
Jerusalem, Israel 97707
02-5813847

יצחק שמואל הלוי ברקוביץ
ראש רשת הכוללים לינת הצדק
סנהדרי'ה המורחבת 113/27
ירושלם ת"ו

Bs"D Jerusalem, 20 Elul 5774

I have read through sections of Rabbi Aryeh Berzansky's *Mesilah* and have found it very inspiring. While the level of stringency among G-d fearing Jews in our generation may very well have exceeded that of our ancestors, our emunah, bitachon and yir'as shamayim are far from that of the most simple Jews generations ago. What is so desperately lacking today is the neshama of Judaism, the emotional connection.

The author's pleasant, unassuming style and unique collection of inspiring stories and insights, evoke feelings of warmth and closeness to our Creator. It is my hope that this work will touch the hearts of many, and that the author will continue to inspire others for many years to come.

בברכה,
יצחק ברקוביץ

בס"ד

Rabbi Zev Leff | הרב זאב לף

Rabbi of Moshav Matityahu
Rosh HaYeshiva—Yeshiva Gedola Matityahu

מרא דאתרא מושב מתתיהו
ראש הישיבה—ישיבה גדולה מתתיהו

D.N. Modiin 71917 Tel: 08–976–1138 טל' Fax: 08–976–5326 פקס' ד.נ. מודיעין 71917

Dear Friends,

I have seen portions of the book "Mesila" by Rabbi Aryeh Berzansky. Although I am not personally acquainted with the author, reliable Talmedei Chachomim attest to his being a Talmid Chochom and Yirei Shomayim.

Rabbi Berzansly presents short to the point essays on the Parshiyos of the Torah and various Moadim. These essays are culled from vaadim he gave in Lakewood Yeshiva in Eretz Yisroel.

I found the material to be interesting, informative, and inspiring. The ideas are based on solid Torah sources and deliver a practical lesson to be implemented in one's life as a Torah Jew.

I commend the author for a quality presentation and recommend "Mesila" to all those who want to enhance their knowledge of and inspiration from, the Parshiyos and Moadim. This book will also provide material for quality Divrei Torah at one's Shabbos and Yom Tov table.

May Hashem provide the author with the wherewithal to continue to merit the community with further Torah works.

Sincerely,
With Torah blessings
Zev Leff
Rabbi Zev Leff

הסכמת הגאון ר' צבי יעקב קרמר שליט"א
ר"מ בישיבת לייקווד באר"י

עש"ק דברים תשע"ד פה ירושלים ע'ה"ק

לדידי נפשי – היושב בסתר לבי – הרה"ג ר' אריה שליט"א מופלג בתורה ומוכתר בנימוסים ודרכי מוסר נו'נ ומוסר "ועדים במוסר" בישיבה הק' דליקווד בא"י

A heartfelt ברכה on the completion of the ספר based on the weekly ועדים given in ישיבת ליקווד in א"י. My family and I always happily anticipate the weekly דברי תורה of הרה"ג רב ארי'ה שליט"א, and now that they are printed in a permanent book form, our שמחה is even greater.

Being a ת"ח of great status, רב ארי'ה is very particular that everything stated in the דברי תורה should comply fully to all דקדוקי הלכה. But even more important, רב ארי'ה שליט"א will not write a "vort" — even if it is sharp and sweet — unless a practical lesson can be learned from the חידוש. רב ארי'ה, adhering to the tradition of the great בעלי מוסר, is continuously working to "grow" and to achieve self-improvement. Therefore, just as his ועדים have a great effect on its listeners, so the practical מוסר derived from his דברי תורה will surely have a profound effect on the reader, as חז"ל say:

דברים היוצאים מן הלב נכנסים אל הלב.

ברכה מעומקא דליבא, שיעלה מעלה מעלה בתורה ומוסה, וירבה חילו לאורייתא, ויזכה להרביץ תורה ומוסה,

כלבבו וכלב אוהבו,

צבי יעקב קרמר

ספר זה יצא לאור

לעילוי נשמת הורינו היקרים

הר"ר נפתלי חיים ב"ר שמחה **הכהן** ז"ל

הלברשטדט

וזוגתו מרת **בלומא** בת ר' שמואל ע"ה

הר"ר אברהם משה ב"ר צבי ז"ל **דובר**

ת.נ.צ.ב.ה.

In memory of my beloved father

Dovid ben Yosef z"l

He taught us that happiness is making other people happy.
He personified kindness.
Always a smile, a chuckle or a little dance.
Everybody loved him.
He loved us more than anything in the world.
I could not have asked for a more perfect father.
I miss you and love you with all my heart.
I hope that we are bringing you much peace.
Love your son,

Aryeh Berzansky

In loving memory of my beloved mother-in-law

Masha Chaya bas Reuwen

MARCY MANNE ob"m.

Her energy was one of vibrancy and joyfulness.
Everybody she met loved her; even strangers wanted to be her friend.

Even in her last difficult years she still managed to inspire people with her upbeat attitude and zest for life.

She was a woman that lived with her dream, no matter what anybody else thought.
A real doer.

May we bring you much peace and comfort.

Love your children and grandchildren.
Aryeh Berzansky

TABLE OF CONTENTS

SEFER SHEMOS

SEFER VAYIKRA

SEFER BAMIDBAR

SEFER DEVORIM

MOADIM

INTRODUCTION

We live in a world that is craving direction and purpose. With the collapse of all the world's ideologies, many people today find themselves with nowhere to turn except for Google. We, the Jewish people, on the other hand, are fortunate to have the ultimate truth, the Torah, in our lives, guiding us every step of the way.

The Torah is more than just a mere rulebook; it teaches us how to live. Its indispensable guidance and wisdom form a *mesilah*, a path, for all of us to tread. This path is of a divine nature and contains the recipe for the ultimate happiness, providing solutions for every situation and leading us to a true and meaningful life.

By learning the *parshiyos* and their commentaries, one can discover for oneself such a path, a *mahalach ha-chaim*.

We can learn the power of giving from Noach, says Rav Dessler, and how to overcome challenges from Yitzchak Avinu, says the Chafetz Chaim. The Ibn Ezra learns from the story of *Yetzias Mitzrayim* how people impose self-limitations upon themselves, and Rav Moshe Feinstein finds guidance on how to raise our children in certain mitzvos.

There is a solution to every quandary and direction for every goal, and it is ours. It is truly the blessing of our lives.

This book is a compilation of lessons for life that I have drawn from the *parshiyos*. My sole intention in writing it is to share with you tiny glimpses of the Torah's beauty. I hope that these lessons will warm your heart as they did mine.

Almost every *d'var torah* has an inspirational story attached to it as well as a lesson for life, thus making it Shabbos-table friendly and a springboard for further thoughts and discussions.

My *tefillah* to Hashem is that we should cherish His Torah that He has so kindly given us, as well as walk its *mesilah*, its path of life, with inspiration and enthusiasm until the Coming of Mashiach, may it occur speedily in our days.

Aryeh Berzansky
Yerushalayim
Elul 5774

ACKNOWLEDGMENTS

If I would start to thank Hashem for everything in my life, my list would never end, but I feel that I should at least begin. Therefore, I would like to express, as a token of appreciation, a few *brachos* that Hashem has showered upon me in relation to this book. Thank You for putting me on the right path, opening my eyes to the beauty of the Torah, giving me the ability to understand it and explain it to others in a clear fashion, and allowing me to be the conduit of such priceless values. Thank You for my *rebbeim*, family, and friends who love me, support me, and have always been there for me.

I would like to thank several individuals who were particularly instrumental in the publication of this book.

Moreinu HaRav HaGaon R. Yaakov E. Schwartzman, Rosh Yeshivas Lakewood Yerushalayim, for creating a Torah environment that I have been able to grow in. It is amazing to witness a true *talmid chacham* in action. The *shiurim* and *shmoozen* I have heard from him have been a true inspiration.

HaRav HaGaon R. Shabsai Black, Rosh Yeshivas Ohr Yaakov, for teaching me how to be a beautiful Jew and imbuing me with all the fundamentals that I have written in this book.

HaRav HaGaon R. Hershy Kramer, Magid Shiur in Yeshivas Lakewood Yerushalayim, for making sure that the Torah ideas expressed in this book are true Torah ideas. He always made himself available to me, and gave me his invaluable support, advice, and guidance.

To Harav HaGaon R. Yaacov Haber, R. Doron Kornbluth, and the whole Mosaica Press staff: your professionalism and patience, together with your guidance, really made it a pleasure to work with you. Thank you for turning a dream into a reality. May Hashem continue to give you much *hatzlachah* and success in bringing Torah to the world.

I would like to thank a special individual for all that he has done. His love for Torah, and in particular *chiddushei Torah*, is something to be admired. May Hashem grant him much *hatzlachah*, *nachas*, and *brachah* in all of his endeavors.

I would like to give a special thank you to R. Yitzchok Elefant. Without his priceless guidance, input, and encouragement, this book would never have happened. His clarity, direction, and power of analysis are nothing less than awesome. I would particularly like to thank him for believing in me until the end. So many times I was ready to throw in the towel, and somehow he managed to get me over each hurdle until I was finally finished.

R. Michoel Dover for his dozens of hours of editing the manuscripts over and over again, as well as his invaluable input.

HaRav Akiva Homnick, HaRav Nachman Marcuson, R. Avraham Weiss and R. Pinchas Yaakov Kohn for proofreading the manuscripts.

R. Yitchchok Goldman for his patience in helping me filter through tens of titles for the book. Although he never liked any of my ideas, he was always there to hear me out, advise me and guide me.

For all the *talmidim* that have come to my *vaadim*. Every *vaad* was another opportunity to further clarify and internalize the ideas expressed in the book.

HaRav Avraham Schwab, HaRav Dovid Slavin, HaRav Geller, and HaRav Grossman for giving me much inspiration and *chizuk* throughout my life.

Mrs. Gavant for doing such a wonderful job at editing parts of the book.

Mrs. Devora Bella Hommel for her input, and Mrs. Chani Abramowitz for creating a wonderful book cover.

Tzodok Abenson for believing in me and teaching me to believe in myself.

Mordechai Hommel for being my first sponsor and helping me with the cover.

Shevach Yisroel Landau for all of his encouragement.

My dad *z"l*, for teaching me that happiness is making other people happy.

My mom. She figured out how to be the best mom in the whole world. Her love, support, concern, advice, and affection make my heart sing.

My wonderful sisters, Zoey and Yocheved, for being so supportive of me and helping me process some of the essays in the book.

My father-in-law, may he be blessed with many happy years, and, *yi'badel bein chaim l'chaim,* my late mother-in-law, for encouraging us and loving us.

My wonderful wife for giving me thousands of hours towards writing this book. In addition, I would like to thank her for giving me the freedom and peace of mind to learn without distractions. Her constant love, support, and affection holds no bounds. She simply takes care of me together with my family. You are such a *brachah* to my life. I can truly say about her, "Yours and mine is hers," because without her it would never have happened.

My children, from whom I learn so much every day. Each and every one of you is so special to me.

May Hashem bless all of you and your families with much *brachah*, *hatzlachah*, *nachas*, *simchas ha'chaim*, and *arichas yomim*.

SEFER BEREISHIS

WHAT ARE OTHER PEOPLE HERE FOR?

PARSHAS BEREISHIS

לֹא טוֹב הֱיוֹת הָאָדָם לְבַדּוֹ (ב, יח)
It is not good that man should be alone.

Nesanel was holding onto one of the younger boy's hands during the *hakafos* of Simchas Torah. After a good round of dancing, the young boy looked up at his "big friend" Nesanel for reassurance and asked, "How am I dancing? Is it okay?" Nesanel smiled and said, "Your dancing is not just okay, it's amazing!" The young boy's face gleamed with self-confidence as he continued to dance until the end of all the *hakafos*.

Adam and Chava were initially created and lived in one body,[1] and only later were they separated and placed into two bodies.[2] Living in one body did not allow them to give selflessly to one another because every time they would give, they would simultaneously be giving to themselves. Only once they were separated was the window of selfless giving open before them.[3]

---

1 They must have been akin to Siamese twins.
2 *Eruvin* 18b: "*Du partzufim nivra'u.*"
3 R. Chaim Friedlander in his *kuntres* to *chasanim*, "*Ve'yadata ke shalom*

Therefore, when Hashem said, "It is not good for man to be alone," He did not mean alone in the literal sense, since Chava was already created together with him in one body. Rather, "alone" meant the inability to give selflessly to another person. The Torah is teaching us that Hashem wants selfless giving because if not, He would have kept Adam and Chava together in one body.[4]

Although the Torah uses the relationship of husband and wife as the catalyst to teach us that we are here to give,[5] nonetheless the principle is true for every relationship. Other people are here for us so that we can selflessly give to them.

Giving can take on many forms. We can give a smile, a helping hand, time, or money. We can give our family and friends the space they need when they need it. We can give a new neighbor a cake or the new *bochur* in yeshiva a warm and hearty welcome. We can also give words of encouragement, or listen to a friend when he or she needs listening to.

Whatever it is, we can't forget that other people are in the world for us to give to them, and in truth, the more we give, the better we will become.

---

b'ohalecha," ch. 1.

4 When Hashem said, "I will make for Adam a helper opposite him," an *ezer kanegdo*, the stress was obviously not on the "helper" aspect, because Adam already had his helper, Chava, attached to him. Rather the stress is meant to be on the aspect of "opposite him." The point was to have his preexisting helper now stand separate and detached from him, thus making them into two entities. (The word *kaneged* is a difficult word to translate in the context of our *pasuk*. Many commentaries do not translate according to its literal meaning of "opposite him.")

5 R. Friedlander, ibid., explains that the relationship between husband and wife is indeed a unique relationship in the aspect of giving.

OUR LOVE FOR MITZVOS

PARSHAS BEREISHIS

וַיַּבְדֵּל בֵּין הַמַּיִם (א, ז)
And He separated the waters.

After a very exhausting Simchas Torah, everybody in the town of Berditchev was sound asleep...except for R. Levi Yitzchok. His incredible love for mitzvos was keeping him awake. He was anxiously awaiting daybreak so that he could once again perform the mitzvah of *tefillin*.[6]

Although such a love and appreciation for mitzvos is beyond our comprehension, we too can love and appreciate mitzvos on our own level. Perhaps the Medrash in our *parshah* can remind us of the magnitude of even one mitzvah, and thus awaken that love and appreciation towards them.

The Medrash tells us that when Hashem separated the lower waters from the upper waters and then lowered them down to earth, they cried profusely.[7] "It is not fair that the upper waters remain in the higher, spiritual worlds close to You, while we have to be lowered down to a materialistic and impure world, far away

6 He did not wear *tefillin* for the week of Succos, since the widespread *minhag* for Ashkenazim is not to wear *tefillin* during the whole week of Succos.

7 *Medrash Rabbah, Bereishis* 5.

from You." Hashem compensated them with the mitzvah of *Nisuch haMayim*.[8]

Now, no matter how great the mitzvah of *Nisuch haMayim* was, it was performed with a small measure of water,[9] only during the seven days of Succos, and only while the Beis Hamikdash stood. How could such a mitzvah compensate all the rivers, streams, lakes, and oceans — "the lower waters" — for all time?

From here we see, says R. Yosef Salant,[10] the magnitude of a mitzvah. When Hashem compensated the lower waters, He gave them something that would raise them to the level of the upper waters. Even though they were in a materialistic and impure world, nonetheless the mitzvah of *Nisuch haMayim* elevated and equaled them to the stature of the upper waters!

Such a Medrash teaches us the value of one mitzvah, and R. Levi Yitzchok of Berditichev personified just that. His love and enthusiasm for mitzvos was something to be admired.

The Vilna Gaon too lived with that love and appreciation. We all are familiar with the story of how he held onto his *tzitzis* as he left this world and cried, "With just a little money we can perform such precious mitzvos like these!"

Knowing that our days are flooded with mitzvos is not enough; it takes a wise man to remember their magnitude and act accordingly. May we too become wise in this aspect and fill our days with mitzvos — things of meaning and worth.

8 The mitzvah of pouring water libations on top of the *Mizbe'ach* during the days of Succos. R. Salant points out that although the lower waters were not satisfied with this mitzvah until Hashem gave them the salt as well, nonetheless in Hashem's eyes it would have been sufficient to give the mitzvah of *Nisuch haMayim* to compensate the lower waters.

9 Three *lugin*. Three *lugin* is about eighteen fluid ounces.

10 In *Be'er Yosef*.

A Mode of Transformation, Not Transportation

Parshas Noach

כִּי מָלְאָה הָאָרֶץ חָמָס מִפְּנֵיהֶם (ו, יג)
The world is filled with grabbers.

Noach and his family tended to all the animals in the *teivah* for an entire year. During that year, they fed tens of thousands of animals, birds, reptiles, and insects their appropriate foods in their appropriate times, without a moment's break. In order to facilitate this tremendous burden of responsibility, Noach and his family had to set aside their own personal lives and interests and focus solely on the needs of the animals. Imagine a nurse who has to maintain a birthing ward for over two thousand hungry newborn babies, all by herself! Such an analogy is really child's play in comparison to what really transpired during that year in the *teivah*. The superhuman powers that they had to muster are incomprehensible.[11]

11 Look in the *Sifsei Chaim, Middos v'Avodas Hashem*, vol. 1, *Olam Chessed Yi'baneh, Vaad* 2.

However, one could ask, why did Hashem put Noach and his family through such turmoil? After all, Chazal[12] tell us that the floodwaters never entered into Eretz Yisroel. Hashem could have steered the *teivah* directly towards Eretz Yisroel, enabling Noach to transport all the animals to a safe haven within a matter of days.

R. Dessler learns from this that the year in the *teivah* was not only a means of transportation, but a goal in itself. He explains that Hashem placed Noach in this situation not only to maintain the animals in the *teivah*, but also to rectify the sin that caused the flood.[13]

Targum Onkeles categorizes the people of that generation as "grabbers." Hence, their sin was selfishness.[14] In the words of R. Dessler, they were "takers." Every single person ignored the needs of everybody else as he indulged solely in his own personal passions, needs, and wants. Such behavior warranted total destruction of the world, because it is the antithesis of *chessed*, which builds the world.[15] *Chessed* means to be concerned for other people's needs to the point that we are willing to put our own personal needs on the side for their sake, and being that the whole generation lacked this, Hashem brought the flood.

Once the flood began and the entire population of the world shrunk down to Noach's family, they were able to turn the world into a world of giving, a world of *chessed*. They lived a life of sheer selflessness, totally ignoring their own personal needs and wants and focusing entirely on the needs of the animals. The monkeys liked bananas at twelve noon and again at seven in the evening. The lions liked their meat first thing in the morning and again around twilight. And so on and so forth. They had to figure out what every animal, bird, reptile, and insect liked, when they liked it, and how much of it they liked, in order to give to them properly.

---

12 *Zevachim* 113b.

13 *Michtav M'Eliyahu*, vol. 2, pg. 155.

14 Because grabbers by definition are selfish people, "*Kei malo ha'aretz chamas*" (*Bereishis* 6:13).

15 Dovid haMelech taught us that *chessed* builds the world, "*Olam chessed yi'baneh*" (*Tehillim* 89:3).

They were not merely transporting animals; they were transforming the world into a world of selfless givers, a world of *chessed*.

Now we can understand why Hashem kept them in the *teivah* for an entire year. The world needed a year of giving, a year of healing, which was the key factor that brought about the salvation.

There is much to learn from the flood. How often do our personal desires drown out the needs of our friends and family? People push and shove to get their seat on the bus or their place in line while leaving others stranded at the wayside. Let us learn from the flood how destructive taking can be, and how healing the power of giving can be. Giving is an extremely powerful tool. Not only does it build the world, it maintains it as well.

Let us partake in this wonderful act by putting ourselves aside for the needs of our wives, friends, or family. Who knows — we might actually like it.

OUR SPIRITUAL INHERITANCE

PARSHAS LECH LECHA

לֶךְ לְךָ מֵאַרְצְךָ... אֶל הָאָרֶץ אֲשֶׁר אַרְאֶךָּ (יב, א)
Go...from your land...to the land that I will show you.

Several years ago, my family and I experienced an incident in the airport that we would never forget. We were traveling back to Eretz Yisroel shortly after 9/11 and when we arrived at Kennedy Airport it looked like a ghost town. There were no lines, no traffic, no pushing and shoving; nothing except the airport staff. However, when we arrived at the terminal for the flights to Tel Aviv, everything seemed to be running as usual, as if the Twin Towers never fell. There was noise and hustle and bustle; hatboxes and handbags were flying about. Everybody seemed anxious and excited to board the plane headed for Eretz Yisroel. Not only that, but our flight was even overbooked with people on standby, eager to get a seat! It was a sight to see and remember.

"Can it be," I thought to myself, "that everybody here did not listen to the news? How can it be that only we continue on with our lives in the wake of the Twin Tower catastrophe, while the rest of the world is petrified from it?" Why were the Jews not fazed by 9/11, while the rest of the world was?

The answer is that we are children of Avraham Avinu. Let us explain.[16]

R. Chaim of Volozhin explains that when a *tzaddik* applies himself, to the best of his abilities, to triumph over a challenge or to acquire a specific attribute or level in his *avodas Hashem*, he carves a spiritual path that enables his children after him to reach those levels without much effort or toil at all.[17] Sometimes those levels could even come naturally to his children. This is what we call a spiritual inheritance. This is one of the reasons why Avraham is called *avinu* — our father, because he gave us a spiritual inheritance.

Many years ago, Avraham Avinu went through a test called *Lech Lecha*. He had to uproot himself from his homeland and travel to a land that was unknown to him at the time. This required a tremendous amount of *emunah* in addition to self-sacrifice on his part. R. Chaim of Volozhin explains that every time Avraham Avinu passed a test, he succeeded in inculcating into the Jewish genes the ability to overcome similar tests in the future. The test of *Lech Lecha* transmitted to his children a passion for Eretz Yisroel. This passion, consciously or subconsciously, has enabled Jews over the centuries to travel on dangerous seas, leave their homelands, or fly a few days after 9/11 in order to realize their dreams of coming to Eretz Yisroel.

The ability to be *moser nefesh*[18] has also become part of our DNA due to Avraham Avinu's *mesiras nefesh*. When Avraham Avinu jumped into the fiery furnace, not only did he attest to his faith in Hashem, but he also carved a pathway for Jews to be *moser nefesh* as well. We have witnessed over the ages thousands of religious Jews who lost their jobs for the sake of *Shabbos kodesh*. Countless Jews from the most secular to the most religious were willing to give up their lives for *kiddush Hashem*. All this can be attributed to the inheritance that we have received from Avraham Avinu. Today, we can say that just as

16 Based on *Michtav M'Eliyahu*, vol. 1, pgs. 8–12.

17 *Ruach Chaim* 5:2.

18 Self-sacrifice.

a spider knows how to spin a web, and a beaver knows how to build a dam, a Jew knows how to be *moser nefesh* for Hashem.[19]

Another example is the test of the famine. When Avraham wholly accepted the hardship of the famine with love, he implanted into our hearts the ability to say *gam zu l'tovah* — to accept all situations with a smile and take on any challenge . Today, it is very rare to find a Jew who is so disheartened from a disaster that he cannot pick himself up and start again. Consequently, we have within us the ability to accept whatever befalls us, as well as the stamina to persevere through any storm. These are only some examples of the hidden riches that we have inherited from Avraham Avinu.

After all that is said and done, an inheritance is worth something only when the beneficiary puts it to good use.[20] We can choose to leave these attributes dormant inside or we can utilize them to our advantage and release them to the world. The decision is up to us.

19 I heard this analogy from R. Moshe Wolfson of Brooklyn.

20 A spiritual inheritance is compared to a long line of zeros. It is worthless unless you put a number before it.

REAL KINDNESS

PARSHAS LECH LECHA

וַיְהִי בִּימֵי אַמְרָפֶל (יד, א)

And it happened in the days of Amraphel.

I think we can all agree that Avraham Avinu was the furthest thing from a fighter or warrior. Most of us would picture him as a superhuman being that personified kindness and compassion. Nonetheless, we find that he not only participated in the war of the kings, but he actually led it. It was a full-scale war that killed hundreds, if not thousands of people!

The answer is that the biggest kindness one can do for the world and for mankind is to do what Hashem wants. Kindness does not mean to be kind to all. Kindness is to bring Godliness into the world, and that is what Avraham did.

THERE IS GIVING AND THEN THERE IS GIVING

PARSHAS VAYEIRA

וַיִּשָּׂא עֵינָיו...וַיָּרָץ לִקְרָאתָם (יח, ב)
He lifted up his eyes...And he ran to greet them.

The Gemara says that the mitzvah of *chessed* is greater than the mitzvah of *tzedakah*.[21] It illustrates this with a number of examples. One is that *tzedakah* can only be done with the poor, whereas *chessed* can be done with the rich and poor alike. The Maharal understands that Chazal are not only teaching us that *chessed* applies in more scenarios than *tzedakah*, rather they are also teaching us that *chessed* is intrinsically greater than *tzedakah*.[22] However, this needs explanation. If both mitzvos are performed in the very same manner, one person giving to another, how can *chessed* be intrinsically greater?

The Maharal writes that it all depends on our motivation behind the mitzvah. If a person is only giving because something is compelling him to do so,[23] such as a nagging phone caller, a guilty

21 *Sotah* 19b.
22 *Nesivos Olam, Nesiv Gemilas Chasadim*, the end of the second chapter.
23 Most people are motivated externally as well as internally together. Our

conscious, peer pressure, or seeing another person suffer,[24] then the giver is performing the mitzvah of *tzedakah* but not the mitzvah of *chessed*. The mitzvah of *chessed*, on the other hand, comes from a self-motivated internal desire to give, share, and help others. There is no external motivation except for the giver's will to give.[25]

This can help us understand why *tzedakah* can only be done with the poor and not the rich. A poor person, with his pains and ailments, motivates givers to give. If the poor person would disappear, then so would the giving. *Tzedakah* cannot be given to the rich because rich people are people who lack nothing. If there is no lack or void that needs to be filled, there is no reason to give and consequently the giver will not give.

Chessed, however, can even be done to people that do not "need" anything, i.e., rich people, because *chessed* starts internally, from the benefactor's desire to give, share, and help others. Even if there is no lack or void to fill, there is always what to give.

An analogy will help crystallize this idea. Reuven always brings extra change with him to give to the poor when he visits the *kosel*. If he is bringing the money because it pains him to see poor people suffering or because he feels guilty when he does not give, then he is fulfilling the mitzvah of *tzedakah* and not the mitzvah of *chessed*.[26]

However, if he had a bit of a loftier intention and would have given the money because he wanted to help others, then he would have elevated his action into a mitzvah of *chessed* as well. Not only would he be rewarded for filling the void of the recipient, which is the mitzvah of *tzedakah*, but he would have also been rewarded handsomely for his desire to help others, which is the enhanced mitzvah of *chessed*.

It is interesting to note that if the recipient was not really a poor

---

question is towards which side of the camp is one leaning. In order to get our definitions clear, we will be referring to the extremes.

24 Look in the *Chovos Halevavos* in his introduction to *Sha'ar Avodas Elokim*.

25 In *yeshivish* terms, we would say *tzedakah* is when the *cheftza* creates the mitzvah, and *chessed* is when the *gavra* creates the mitzvah.

26 Of course, *tzedakah* is an awesome mitzvah. Chazal (*Bava Basra* 8b) tell us that the mitzvah of *tzedakah* not only can eradicate a *gezeirah ra*, it can even save people from death. We are only talking in relation to *chessed*.

person, but a crook, the giver did not perform the mitzvah of *tzedakah* because by definition *tzedakah* means to fill the void of the recipient. Here, there was no void to fill, since the "poor person" was not missing anything. Whereas if he gave with the intention to help others, he would have merited reward for the mitzvah of *chessed* that he did perform.

This is what happened with Avraham Avinu in this week's *parshah*. He gave food and drink to angels who did not need food and drink. Consequently, there was no mitzvah of *tzedakah* performed. However, since Avraham gave because he wanted to help others, he did perform the mitzvah of *chessed*.[27]

Now we can finally understand why *chessed* is in a class on its own. One who performs the mitzvah of *chessed* does so solely with the intention to give, share, and help others. It is truly a selfless mitzvah, whereas the mitzvah of *tzedakah*, since it is an externally motivated mitzvah, is not a selfless mitzvah; on the contrary, if one gave in order to remove his pain or guilty conscience, it has traces of selfishness within it.

Therefore, since *chessed* is an act of selflessness and *tzedakah* is an act of selfishness, we can honestly say that *chessed* is truly a greater mitzvah — not only quantitatively, but even qualitatively. We can also understand how two people could perform the very same act of giving, and one will have done the mitzvah of *tzedakah*, while the other will have fulfilled the mitzvah of *chessed* as well; it all depends on what motivated him!

27 Look in *Michtav M'Eliyahu*, vol. 4, pg. 1.

The Unanswered Tefillah

Parshas Vayeira

הַמְכַסֶּה אֲנִי מֵאַבְרָהָם...וְאַבְרָהָם הָיוֹ יִהְיֶה לְגוֹי גָּדוֹל וְעָצוּם (יח, יז–יח)

How can I hide what I am doing to Sodom from Avraham… Avraham will become a great and mighty nation.

Shimon was in critical condition. His good friend Eliyahu had poured out his heart, asking Hashem to save his dear friend's life. Unfortunately, after three weeks of *tefillos*, Shimon passed away. There is no doubt, writes R. Shimshon Pincus, that Eliyahu's *tefillos* helped Shimon in more ways than we could imagine,[28] but aside from helping Shimon, Eliyahu's *tefillos* actually helped Eliyahu's little brother Yossi as well.[29]

Three months after Shimon's passing, Eliyahu's little brother Yossi was severely injured in a car accident on *erev* Shabbos, in Lakewood, New Jersey. Eliyahu did not hear about the crash because he was in Eretz Yisroel and it was already Shabbos. Hashem took Eliyahu's three-month-old *tefillos* and used them to save Yossi's life. Sunday morning, Eliyahu received a call from his family in Lakewood, telling

28 Perhaps Shimon was able to live longer or had less pain.
29 Based on R. Shimshon Pincus, *Shearim Be'Tefillah*, ch. *Eitor* 6.

him not to panic, but that Yossi was severely injured in a car crash on *erev* Shabbos and *baruch Hashem* he is going to be just fine.

The Medrash teaches us that not all *tefillos* work instantaneously.[30] Some help after three days, some after thirty days, some only after thirty years, and some even more. Hashem with His infinite wisdom knows where and when to use them. Our job is just to create them.

Hashem wanted to inform Avraham Avinu about the imminent destruction of Sodom. He said, "How can I hide what I am doing to Sodom from Avraham? Avraham will become a great and mighty nation." The Dubner Maggid is bothered by the juxtaposition of these two *pesukim*.[31] The implications are that Hashem had to tell Avraham that He was going to destroy Sodom since a great nation was going to emerge from Avraham. What is the connection?

The Dubner Maggid explains that although Hashem knew that Sodom's destruction was imminent and unavoidable, nonetheless He still wanted Avraham Avinu to *daven* for their salvation. That is because Hashem was not interested in the salvation of Sodom per se; rather Hashem was interested in Avraham's *tefillos*. Let us explain.

Hashem knew the power that lay in Avraham's *tefillos* and wanted to store them up in his flask of *tefillos* for a later date and time when Avraham Avinu's children, Klal Yisroel, would need them.[32] Hashem knew that as soon as He would tell Avraham about Sodom, Avraham would pour his heart and soul out in prayer for their salvation and safety. Hashem was saving up those *tefillos* for a time when Avraham would not be around to *daven* on our behalf.

The Dubner Maggid explains this idea with a parable. Two people entered a children's clothing store. The older one was measuring every item of clothing to make sure that it would fit, while the younger one was just buying whatever looked good. The older man asked the younger man in astonishment, "How can you buy clothes for your children without first knowing if they fit?" The younger one replied, "*Baruch Hashem*, I have a house filled with lots of boys. If

30 *Medrash Shmuel* 4, which is brought in *Chayei Olam*, ch. 28.

31 The Dubner Maggid is also brought in *Shearim Be'Tefillah*, ibid.

32 *Tehillim* 56:9, "*Sima demasee b'nodech.*"

this shirt doesn't fit one, it will fit another. And if it does not fit any of them today, it will fit one of them tomorrow."

Just like Hashem saved the *tefillos* of Avraham in His "flask of *tefillos*" for a time when they will be needed, explains the Dubner Maggid, so too Hashem saves the *tefillos* of Klal Yisroel for the time when they will be needed as well.

A Jew must know that there is no such thing as a *tefillah* going to waste. Every time a Jew pours his heart out to Hashem, his *tefillah* is heard.[33] Hashem takes it and places it in His "flask of *tefillos*" where it will wait to be used in its appropriate time.

33 It is included in the *brachah* that Yitzchok Avinu gave to Yaakov Avinu. See Rashi to *Parshas Chukas* (*Bamidbar* 20:16) s.v. "*Vayishma Koleinu*."

HASHEM CHANGED THE SCRIPT

PARSHAS CHAYAI SARA

וַיֹּאמַר עֶבֶד אַבְרָהָם אָנֹכִי (כד, לד)
And he said, "I am Avraham's *eved* (slave)."

We all dream. Some people dream of becoming the next *Gadol haDor*. Others dream of getting the prospective job or *shidduch* that is on the horizon, and others dream that their children will become big *tzaddikim* and *tzidkanious*. What happens when Hashem does not give us what we dreamed for? How do we feel? Most of us probably get down, some declare *gam zu l'tovah*, and others actually bless Hashem for the bad just as they bless Him for the good.

Eliezer *eved* Avraham[34] also dreamed just like all of us. If we could look into his heart, we would see no more than one dream: that Yitzchok Avinu would marry *his* daughter. However, that dream never manifested. Avraham told Eliezer that since his daughter was from a cursed nation (a nation of *avadim*), and Avraham's son Yitzchok was from a blessed nation, therefore their children could not marry.[35]

34 Eliezer was Avraham's slave.
35 Rashi to *Bereishis* 24:39, *"Beni baruch, v'atah arur, v'ain ha'arur midabek b'baruch."*

To make matters worse, Avraham had asked him to go to the city of Charan to find a wife for Yitzchok. Such a task should have been like salt on his wound. He should have been insulted, shattered, and gone begrudgingly.

However, Eliezer carried out Avraham's request with enthusiasm and gusto! This was evident from the miracles that he experienced along the way. His *tefillos* were answered instantly when he *davened* to find Yitzchok's match and, as we know, only *tefillos* that come from the deepest depths of one's heart are answered instantly. Additionally, he had *kefitzas ha-derech*,[36] which only happens to one who acts with alacrity and sincerity.

Now, even if we could understand Eliezer's enthusiasm to carry out his master's request, but to introduce himself to Lavan and Besuel as "I am Avraham's *eved* (slave)," which implied that he was from a cursed nation, is astonishing. What happened to his dignity and pride? Where were his hurt feelings? After all, it was because he was an *eved* from that nation of *avadim* that his dreams crumbled right before his eyes.

R. Yechezkel Levenstein opens our eyes to the secret.[37] Eliezer was happy with who he was; he was *sameach b'chelko*. He understood and believed that every single person has a specific job and purpose in the world for which only he is designated. As soon as he heard from Avraham that the cursed and blessed could not unite, he understood that his daughter was not meant for Yitzchok. Nothing more needed to be said. This revelation clarified for him what his real purpose was: to be "Eliezer *eved* Avraham." That clarity propelled him towards his job of becoming the best "*eved* Avraham" that he could be. This is how he was able to run with such enthusiasm to Charan and *daven* with all his heart for Yitzchok's future wife Rivka.

When Eliezer *eved* Avraham discovered that his dream did not fit into Hashem's master plan, he accepted his new lot unconditionally and began working on what Hashem had actually planned for him.

---

36 Shortening of the way.

37 From the writings of R. Yechezkel Levinstein, which are brought in *Lekach Tov, Chaim Shel Torah*, vol. 3, pg. 72.

This brought him happiness and tranquility.[38]

Eliezer *eved* Avraham is a living example of *bitachon* for all of us. We all have hopes and dreams. If for some reason Hashem does not grant us our dreams, we must remind ourselves that He is taking care of us and that somehow our dreams did not fit into His master plan. When Eliezer realized that Yitzchok was not going to marry his daughter, he discovered his purpose right underneath his nose and he bore it with pride.

Hashem has something special planned for all of us and it is hiding in our own backyard. As soon as we discover it, we will find happiness and tranquility within ourselves.

---

38 Korach, however, was the antithesis of Eliezer. His dream was to become the leader of Klal Yisroel. The only problem was that Hashem had a different plan for him. Korach did not budge from trying to bring his dream to fruition. He unsuccessfully devoted his efforts in trying to carve this new path, ignoring the path that Hashem had already paved. As a result, he never found happiness and tranquility. See *Parshas Korach*.

PERSEVERANCE

PARSHAS TOLDOS

וַיַּחְפְּרוּ עַבְדֵי יִצְחָק בַּנָּחַל. . . (כו, יט)
And Yitzchok's servants dug wells.

In 1989, an earthquake flattened Armenia, killing over 30,000 people in less than four minutes. A father rushed to the school where his son was supposed to be, only to discover it crumbled before his very eyes. As he looked at the pile of debris, tears fell from his eyes. The situation looked bleak, but he was hopeful. He rushed to where he thought his son's classroom would have been and started to dig. He heard other parents crying and screaming over their lost children, but it did not faze him. The fire chief tried to pull him off the debris, saying, "Fires and explosions are breaking out everywhere. You are in danger! Go home!" He proceeded with determination for eight...twelve...twenty-four...thirty-six hours... Then, in the thirty-eighth hour, he pulled back a boulder and heard his son's voice: "Dad, is that you? There are fourteen of us left out of thirty-three. We are scared, hungry, and thirsty. When the building collapsed, it made a wedge, like a triangle, and we were saved."

Life has its share of hurdles and roadblocks. Sometimes we create our own hurdles by thinking that we are insufficient or incapable of accomplishing a certain task that we are truly capable of achieving. Rabbeinu Bachya writes that when he first considered writing the *Chovos Halevavos*, he felt inadequate to produce such a work.[39] Consequently, he almost stopped himself from putting together one of the most important classical *mussar* masterpieces of all time. We are, at times, our own biggest enemy and hurdle.

Yitzchok Avinu ran into many hurdles when attempting to redig the wells that his father had dug. This could have brought his project to an immediate standstill. Either the *Pelishtim* fought with him over the wells he dug or he found them to be dried out. Whatever it was, he persisted until he found wells with water that he was able to use peacefully.

There is something more powerful than any hurdle, and that is the desire to reach the goal.[40] A famed American executive was in line with what R. Dessler wrote when he said, "Obstacles are what we see when we take our eyes off the goal."[41]

Many people start projects; very few people actually finish them. The distinction is clear: the people who truly want to succeed will succeed. The more a person is determined to finish his project and achieve his goal, the less the obstacle will obstruct his view. Obviously, nothing can happen without Hashem's will, but at the same time, nothing will happen unless we make it happen.

When R. Aharon Kotler decided to create a *Torah liShmah* environment in America, all the odds were against him. He ran into many obstacles and yet he still persevered! He succeeded because he was determined to implement his goal. That determination enabled him to see beyond all obstacles that stood in his way. Today in *yeshivos*, the best *bochurim* by far are the ones who want to succeed, and I am sure that it is like that with the rest of the world as well.

Life has its difficulties and hurdles, but instead of giving up from discouragement and despair when they come our way, we must try

---

39 Look in the introduction to the *Chovos Halevavos*.

40 *Chafetz Chaim* on the Torah.

41 Look in *Michtav M'Eliyahu*, vol. 1, pg. 61. That famed American executive was Henry Ford.

and try again to overcome them until we finally succeed.[42] Don't allow the obstacle to obstruct your vision of what you can accomplish. Desire a goal and pursue it intently! This secret can give a person the determination to climb over any hurdle that comes his way.

42 *Chafetz Chaim* on the Torah.

DO NOT FORGET TO ASK

PARSHAS VAYETZEI

הַפַּעַם אוֹדֶה אֶת ה' (כט, לה)

This time I will give thanks to Hashem.

Leah Imeinu was especially grateful to Hashem for her fourth child. She had prophesized that twelve *shevatim* would emerge from Yaakov Avinu's four wives. Presuming that all the wives would have an equal share, each one should have given birth to three *shevatim*. When Leah gave birth to her fourth son and received "more than her share," she felt extremely appreciative. To express this appreciation she named him "Yehudah." (*Yehudah,* יהודה, is a compound word made up of the word "thanks" — הודה, and Hashem's name — י-ה , meaning "Thank you Hashem.")[43]

However, with all her appreciation and gratitude towards Hashem, the *pasuk* ends on a negative note: "She stopped having children." This implied that since she thanked Hashem, she stopped giving birth, which requires an explanation. Why should she lose the privilege of having more *shevatim* because she thanked Hashem for having her fourth child?

---

43 This attribute of thanksgiving brought her descendants like Dovid haMelech and the prophet Doniel who also personified the attribute of thanking. See *Bereishis Rabbah* 71:5.

The Tur on Chumash offers the following explanation. Her thanking Hashem was not the problem; the problem was that she did not ask for more.[44] The Gemara tells us that when a Jew thanks Hashem for the past, he should simultaneously be asking Hashem for the future.[45] Receiving "more than her share" created a certain sense of fulfillment, which caused her not to ask for more *shevatim*, and as a result, "she stopped having children."[46]

The Torah is teaching us something astonishing. Even if Hashem is ready and willing to give a person something as precious as children, if the person does not ask for it, he will not get it.[47] Hashem can give whenever He wants. However, He wants us to ask Him, and only when we will ask Him will we receive. Leah did not ask for more children and therefore she stopped having children.[48]

A Chassidish *rebbe* once asked his Chassidim at a *tisch*, "Who here would like to be a rich man?" Three raised their hands. Shortly afterwards their businesses flourished, making the three of them multi-millionaires.

Unlike people, our Father in Heaven wants us to ask Him for everything, all the time. Even as we appreciate what He has granted us, we are supposed to turn to Him and ask for His continued help and support.

Whether it is wisdom, healthy, prosperity, or to see the final redemption, don't forget to ask.

---

44 Look in the *Tur* 29:35.

45 *Brachos* 54a: Ben Azai said [to] give thanks on the past and cry on the future.

46 Later on, she earned the privilege to have two more *shevatim*.

47 Obviously, Hashem gives to millions of people things without them even asking. For example, a baby has food and support from his family even though he or she never asked Hashem for help. Nonetheless, there are things that Hashem will only give us if we ask Him.

48 Even though later in the *parshah* Leah did merit more children, Yissachar and Zevulun, she had to work very hard to once again merit the gift of giving birth to more *shevatim*.

YAAKOV'S PREVALENT FEARS

PARSHAS VAYISHLACH

הַצִּילֵנִי נָא מִיַּד אָחִי, מִיַּד עֵשָׂו (לב, יב)

Please [Hashem] save me from the hand of my brother, from the hand of Eisav.

Before Yaakov Avinu met up with Eisav after being separated from him for so many years, he pleaded to Hashem, "Please save me from the hand of my brother, from the hand of Eisav." The Beis Halevi points out a redundancy in Yaakov's plea. Why did Yaakov ask Hashem to save him from "his brother" and then again from "Eisav"? He only had one brother; one prayer would have been sufficient.

The Beis Halevi explains that Yaakov Avinu foresaw one of two inevitably disastrous situations happening. Either Eisav would attempt to kill him because of the past, or he would forgive him on the past and try to reunite. Yaakov was apprehensive of both situations. If the meeting resulted in a friendship, this so-called friendship would force Yaakov to compromise on his *Yiddishkeit,* killing him spiritually. The other choice, Eisav's hatred, would have brought him and his family to an immediate death. Yaakov directed his *tefillos* towards these two fears.

First, he appealed to Hashem to save him "from the hand of his brother" — referring to the brother who might actually love him and would want to befriend him. Then he appealed to Hashem to save him "from the hand of Eisav" — referring to the Eisav who wanted to kill him.

The *pasuk* says that Yaakov was very frightened and distressed.[49] The Beis Halevi explains that he was frightened for his life on the chance that Eisav would kill him, and he was distressed on the chance that Eisav would want to befriend him.

In actuality, Hashem saved Yaakov from both fears. When Eisav finally saw Yaakov, his feelings of hatred were miraculously replaced with feelings of love — so much so that he wanted to travel and live with Yaakov. However, even that never happened, as the *pasuk* says, "On that [very] day that they met, Eisav continued on his way towards Se'ir [and Yaakov went his way]."[50] Hashem saved Yaakov Avinu from both of his fears: "his brother's" friendship and from "Eisav's" hatred.

The fears that Yaakov had are very real and prevalent even today. Chazal tell us that what happens to our *avos* is a sign of what will happen to the Jewish people.[51] The nations, whether consciously or subconsciously, have adopted Eisav's philosophy. They have hatred towards *Yiddishkeit* and *Yidden*. Either they want us to mingle among them in order to bring assimilation, or they want to annihilate us.

We saw this recently with the *churban* of European Jewry how they tried to annihilate us, and today we can see how we are rapidly losing thousands of Jews to assimilation, *Hashem yerachem*. Regrettably so, they will continue trying to prod us until Mashiach comes.

The Beis Halevi explains that Yaakov's fear for "Eisav's friendship" was more distressing in its consequences than the thought of an imminent death. This is because such a friendship can put a strain on one's *avodas Hashem*, as well as bring spiritual annihilation, which

49 *Bereishis* 32:8.

50 Ibid., 33:16.

51 *Maaseh avos siman l'banim*.

is catastrophic. That is why Yaakov asked Hashem to save him from "his brother" before he asked to be saved from "Eisav."

Let us continue in Yaakov's ways, and *daven* that we are saved "from the hand of his brother, from the hand of Eisav," from annihilation and assimilation, and let us hope that Hashem will end this long bitter *galus* speedily in our days.

EVEN A GESTURE CAN BE WORTH MILLIONS

PARSHAS VAYESHEV

וַיַּצִּלֵהוּ מִיָּדָם (לז, כא)
He rescued him from their hand.

The Vilna Gaon's wife and her friend were collecting *tzedakah*. As they were walking, they saw a rich man riding on his horse and buggy. The Vilna Gaon's wife waved her hand to catch his attention. Unfortunately, he drove off without giving them a donation. After her friend had passed away, she visited the Vilna Gaon's wife in a dream, and told her something astonishing: "That act of raising your hand earned you a million more times reward than I received for not raising my hand!"

Reuven convinced his brothers to put Yosef into a pit instead of actually killing him. The Medrash writes that if Reuven would have known that this event was going to be inscribed into the Torah for eternity, he would have carried Yosef on his shoulders straight to his father's house![52]

R. Aharon Kotler explains that although Reuven understood and appreciated the value of a mitzvah, he never fathomed that

52 *Vayikra Rabbah* 34:8.

his actions would have had such rippling effects.[53] Not only was his act incorporated into the Torah for all of eternity, but anytime someone wants to learn this *parshah*, he has to make *bircas haTorah* beforehand. In addition to that, every word of this *parshah* will bring eternal reward to the one who learns it, as well as bring life to the world, just like the rest of the Torah.

Reuven thought that he was saving his little brother Yosef, when in reality he was saving the great Yosef haTzadik and the entire world at the same time. Eventually, Yosef became the deputy of Mitzrayim and the sole provider of food for the entire world during the years of famine. Surely, Reuven never dreamed that his act of salvation would have brought about such an incredible result.

The Medrash continues:[54] "Had Aharon haKohen known that Hashem took note of how joyous he was for his [younger] brother Moshe's good fortune and success, he would have greeted Moshe with an orchestra [and] dancing. Had Boaz known what Hashem was going to write down about him when he fed Rus those few barley kernels, he would have fed her fattened luscious lambs!"

Aside from having their acts recorded for all eternity, there were other colossal rippling effects. From Boaz's act came Dovid haMelech and the Mashiach, and because of Aharon's act of love the *Choshen* rested on his chest.

(It is important to note that we are not judging these Torah giants. Their levels of saintliness and greatness go far beyond our comprehension. We are merely just trying to learn from them on our level in order to better ourselves).

As for us, the Medrash is trying to get us to do mitzvos with the utmost enthusiasm by showing us some of the hidden cosmic repercussions that lie beneath every act that we do. Every act has the power to build worlds! This is also true for every one of us, as the Medrash concludes, "When a person does a mitzvah, Eliyahu haNavi and Mashiach write it down and Hashem signs on it!"

53 *Mishnas Rebbi Aharon*, vol. 3, pg. 192.

54 *Rus Rabbah* 5:6.

Chazal teach us that for every single second that a person remains quiet (when wanting to scream), he creates for himself a world that even the highest of high angels cannot comprehend.[55] That means if he held back from screaming for seven seconds, he just created seven colossal worlds that are beyond comprehension. This is true even if he screams the eighth second! Even the smallest acts are enormous!

One time R. Chaim Shmulevitz *zt"l* was giving a *shiur* to a small group of *bochurim* with the same *bren*[56] as if thousands were attending. They asked him how he was able to do it. He replied, "What do you mean? I am giving a *shiur* to thousands, since everyone here is going to have *talmidim* and they will have *talmidim*, in the thousands." This great man was able to envision the future in front of his very own eyes.[57]

We are fortunate to have this twenty-twenty hindsight. Let's not forget how precious and valuable a simple act of kindness or any good act, for that matter, can be — not only for today or even for tomorrow, but also for tomorrow's tomorrow, and for all eternity.

55 A *Medrash* that is quoted in the *Igeres haGra*.

56 Enthusiasm.

57 Look in *Chovos Halevavos, Sha'ar Ahavas Hashem*, ch. 6, about bringing people closer to Hashem.

THE MASTER PLANNER

PARSHAS MIKEITZ

לָמָּה הֲרֵעֹתֶם לִי (מג, ו)
Why did you treat me so ill?

Many people would come to Yeshivas Slutzk looking for a *shidduch* for their daughters. Most of them were offering very generous dowries, including beautiful apartments, for the best *bochurim* in the yeshiva. Eventually, all the best *bochurim* became *chasanim* and received their apartments, except for R. Shach. Although he was by far one of the best *bochurim* in the yeshiva, both in his consistency and in his understanding, for some reason he was one of the last *bochurim* of his caliber to find his *shidduch*. And even when he did find his *shidduch*, he did not receive any dowry.[58]

After the wedding, R. Shach and his *rebbitzen* moved into his *shver's* apartment to share a room with his brothers-in-law. They split the room with a dividing curtain. His brothers-in-law slept on one side of the curtain and R. Shach and his *rebbitzen* on the other. Although his colleagues felt for him because they had their luxurious apartments and R. Shach did not, nonetheless R. Shach was very

58 He married the niece of the Rosh Yeshiva, R. Isser Zalman Meltzer.

content. He had his most precious things: the Torah and a wife to support him in it.

Shortly thereafter, the war broke out and the Nazis conquered Poland. The Polish ran for their lives to Lithuania and whoever else was able to run ran. Since R. Shach and his *rebbitzen* did not have an apartment "tying them down," they were able to pick themselves up, leave Poland and save their lives. From Poland, they went to Vilna and from Vilna to Eretz Yisroel. His friends and colleges, however, found it tremendously difficult to pull away from their beautiful apartments, and unfortunately, when they finally did, for most of them it was too late. In retrospect, their apartments were their biggest downfall, but for R. Shach, not having an apartment was his salvation.

No matter how far we can see, we still fall short of seeing the whole picture.

The Medrash also teaches us this lesson with Yaakov Avinu. (It is important to note that we cannot make any judgments of Yaakov Avinu. His level of saintliness and greatness is very far beyond our comprehension. We are merely just trying to learn from him on our levels in order to better ourselves).

Yaakov Avinu's hardships and suffering weighed very heavy on his heart, in particular the loss of Yosef. The Medrash tells us that Hashem was somewhat disappointed in Yaakov for living with such a weight on his heart. "I [Hashem] am busy coronating his son over the whole of Mitzrayim and he feels that he is being treated bitterly?"[59]

What seemed to be R. Shach's misfortune was his biggest blessing, and what seemed to be his colleagues' blessing was their biggest misfortune. Our job is not to understand why the darkness is good; it is to believe that it is good and to accept it lovingly.[60]

59 Look in the *Medrash Rabbah* 91:10.

60 The essay was taken from *Lulei So'rascha Sha'ashueye*, courtesy of the author HaRav Asher Bergman *shlita*, a grandson of Maran Harav Shach *zt"l*.

BURST WITH JOY

PARSHAS VAYIGASH

וַיַּעַל לִקְרַאת יִשְׂרָאֵל אָבִיו גֹּשְׁנָה, וַיֵּרָא אֵלָיו (מו, כט)

(Yosef) went up to greet Yisroel, his father, in Goshen. And he appeared before him.

It was the bottom of the ninth inning and the bases were loaded. Shay, a special needs child, was up to bat. He could barely hold the bat — let alone hit the ball. The situation looked bleak and the tension was growing by the minute. One of Shay's teammates came to help him. The pitcher gently threw the ball and Shay actually hit it towards third base. The third baseman intentionally watched it roll right by and everybody began to scream, "Run, Shay, run!" Shay was so excited that he ran right past first base into right field. They yelled out again, "Run, run to second base!" and so he did until he finally made it home. Shay hit a home run and won the game! The boys picked him up and carried him off the field. "You won the game, Shay, you won the game!" They all cheered and Shay's heart was bursting with joy for the first time in his life.

Chances are that the losing team's hearts participated in that joy too. That is the power of selfless giving. It creates feelings of joy for the recipient and the giver alike. You know when it is happening when your nostrils start to flare and you feel a burst of energy inside that brings you to tears of joy.

Of course, we are not supposed to give in order to get, but it is important to know that such feelings exist, because without such knowledge, one's attribute of selfishness can get the better end of him and never let him even begin to seek out how to give, share, and care for others. Consequently, those potentially joyful opportunities will pass him by, like two ships passing in the darkness of the night unnoticed.

In order to be able to give selflessly, one has to be willing to put one's own needs on the side for others. The Alter of Kelm writes that Avraham, Yitzchok, Yaakov, Yosef, Moshe, and Dovid chose to be shepherds for that very purpose.[61] They wanted to create for themselves an environment conducive to selflessness, and since a shepherd must constantly leave his own needs for the needs of his flock, they all decided to become shepherds.

The Medrash crystallizes the point. Moshe Rabbeinu spent three days and nights looking for a lost sheep. When he finally found it, he picked it up and carried it on his shoulders all the way back to the flock. Moshe understood the sheep's feelings and acted accordingly. He understood that after being alone for three days and nights, the sheep must be very scared and hungry. "Let me pick you up," he thought, "and take you home."[62] Moshe was able to see its pain because he was trained, as a shepherd, in selflessness.

Conversely, somebody who cannot see beyond his personal interests would have most probably viewed the situation very differently. "Hey, do you know that I've been running after you for three days and nights; I haven't slept or eaten properly and am completely exhausted? Get back to the flock right now!"

Helping others means putting personal interests aside, just as Moshe Rabbeinu and the "losing team" did. Once a person can see the needs of others, the window of opportunity — to give, share,

---

61 Look in *Chochmah U'mussar*, vol. 1, ch. 2.

62 *Shemos Rabbah* 2:2, which is brought in *Sifsei Chaim, Moadim*, vol. 3, pg. 163.

and even make the recipient's heart, along with his own, burst with joy — opens before him. This window could generate a giving so precious and powerful that it might in fact change the recipient's life forever, just as it did with Shay. More than that, it could change the giver's life, too.

We can see in our *parshah* how Yosef personified this attribute. Imagine how anxious Yosef was to see his father after not seeing him for twenty-two years. When the momentous occasion of being reunited finally arrived, the *pasuk* tells us that Yosef "appeared" to his father, not that he "saw" his father.[63]

R. Naftali Trop explains that Yosef was interested in giving his father the pleasure of seeing him, while his own personal pleasure in seeing his father was inconsequential.[64] Here was an opportunity where personal desires would not conflict with the wants of the recipient, his father, nonetheless he still wanted that moment to be purely for his father's pleasure, not his.

In the beginning of next week's *parshah*, we see again how Yosef was able to disregard his own personal desires for the sake of others. When Yaakov became ill, Efrayim was sent to inform Yosef of his father's illness. The *Daas Zekainim* explains why Yosef himself was not there by his father's side.[65] Yosef was apprehensive to see his father after being reunited. Perhaps Yosef would have been compelled to tell Yaakov that his brothers sold him, which might have resulted in Yaakov cursing them.

(Once again, it is important to note that we are not judging these Torah giants. Their levels of saintliness and greatness go far beyond our comprehension. We are merely just trying to learn from them on our level in order to better ourselves).

This was a tremendous self-sacrifice for Yosef. He was his father's *talmid muvhak*.[66] Before he was sold, he spent every waking moment learning Torah with his father, and now, during the last seventeen

---

63 *Va'yerah elav*.

64 This is brought in *Chayei Mussar*, vol. 2, pg. 189.

65 48:1.

66 Star disciple.

years of his father's life, he refrained from continuing the most precious of his desires — Torah learning with his father — in order to protect his brothers. This is a prime example of a giant in Klal Yisroel, a person who is completely willing to put himself on the side for somebody else.

It is not easy to see past the "blindfold" of our own personal wants into the needs of others. However, those who succeed in doing so have the ability to make people's hearts burst with joy, along with their own, just as the losing team did. May we all make it past that "blindfold" and be there for others the way a Jew is supposed to be.

REACTING CORRECTLY

PARSHAS VAYECHI

פַּחַז כַּמַּיִם אַל תּוֹתַר (מט, ד)

Haste like water, do not take more.

Little four-year-old Dovi surprised his father with a giant "peanut butter and jelly" bear hug on his freshly dry-cleaned pants as soon as he walked through the door. If Dovi's father does not think before he reacts, he might respond in a way that will leave little Dovi flustered, wondering why his father does not love his hugs — or him for that matter.

Many things trigger us off every day. If we are not careful to think before we react, we might regret our reactions later on in time.

(When referring to the *avos*, *shevatim*, Moshe Rabbeinu and the like, we must know that their greatness is far beyond our comprehension. They were giants in spirituality and were on much higher levels than we could ever imagine. When the Torah says that they did wrong, we must understand that it is wrong to their standards, not to ours. According to our definition of wrong, their wrongs would not even register. Nonetheless, we must learn from the Torah and its narrative by applying them to ourselves in order that we can grow.[67])

67 Look in the *Sifsei Chaim*, introduction to *Bereishis*.

In our *parshah*, Yaakov reveals to Reuven the attribute that cost him the birthright, the kingship, and the priesthood. That attribute was impetuosity — acting without forethought.[68]

Yaakov said to Reuven, "Impulsiveness is like water." R. Yeruchem Levovits understands that just as water goes wherever it is led — if a dam cracks, the water will seep out, or if a cup tips over, the water will spill out — so too a person who has the attribute of impetuosity will go wherever he is led.[69] It is almost like a reflex, an automatic reaction without prior thought.

The way to rise above acting impulsively is to act with forethought, and the secret to that is *menuchas hanefesh* (peace of mind and soul). The Alter of Kelm taught us that *menuchas hanefesh* puts a person in control of himself and his actions, and thus enables him to think clearly before acting and reacting. Consequently, with a little forethought, a person can turn his actions and reactions into constructive and positive ones.

In our aforementioned story, if Dovi's father would have simply reacted without forethought, he might have said, "Hey, what are you doing? Don't you know that these are my freshly cleaned pants?" and left little Dovi hurt and confused. However, with a little forethought, he could have refrained and seen his little four-year-old son running to give him a bundle of love and would have responded with love in return.

Let's take another example. Shimon couldn't find one of his shoes on his way out to the last *Minchah*. When he discovered that Dina, his five-year-old daughter, was using it for her pretend shoe store, Shimon lost control and flared up and barked at his five-year-old daughter, "How dare you take my shoe! Don't ever touch my shoes again!"

---

68 R. Eliyahu Lopian explains that Reuven forfeited these privileges not because of what he did, but because of what caused him to do what he did, i.e., the attribute of haste and impulsiveness. After Rachel Imeinu passed away, Yaakov moved his bed into Bilhah's tent. Reuven viewed this as an outrage towards his mother, Leah Imeinu, and reacted on impulse. He hastily moved Yaakov's bed into his mother's tent to defend her honor. He did this so spontaneously that he did not even ask his father.

69 *Daas Torah*.

With a little forethought, however, he might have understood that his daughter had no intention to cause him pain, and would have channeled his reaction towards bettering himself by putting away his shoes in their proper place the next time.

Impulsiveness can rob us of the good messages and feelings that we would like to relay to our friends, family, children, and even ourselves. The key is to have the *menuchas hanefesh* — that peace of mind to be able to think, even for a moment, before one reacts.

If one finds himself reacting in ways that are unfavorable to him when somebody takes his parking place, or his baby wakes him up at three in the morning, it just means that he has not yet perfected restraint. It is true that all it takes is a moment's reflection before responding, but "all it takes" is a life's work. What we must remember is that we are not like water, which has no restraint or control over its actions and reactions, but that we are capable of controlling them and choosing how to act and react. We can even make the decision to react in a positive way — even if the situation prompts negativity.

SEFER SHEMOS

ACHIEVING THE UNACHIEVABLE

PARSHAS SHEMOS

וַתִּשְׁלַח אֶת אֲמָתָהּ וַתִּקָּחֶהָ (ב, ה)

And she extended her arm,[70] and she took it.

Did you ever wonder how some people can walk barefoot on broken glass or karate-chop ten bricks with their bare hands? What about the mother who picked up a car all by herself to save her trapped child from underneath it? R. Chaim Shmuelevitz writes that we all actually have such superhuman strengths deep down inside of us.[71] We inherited them from Adam haRishon.

Before the sin of the *eitz hadaas*, Chazal tell us that Adam haRishon was able to touch the heavens as well as reach both ends of the universe.[72] They were not referring to his physical dimensions, says R. Shmuelevitz, but rather to his innate superhuman strengths. He had the ability to go beyond time and space, as well as to achieve the unachievable.

70 Based on what Chazal say. Look in Rashi there.

71 *Sichos Mussar* 31:5.

72 *Sanhedrin* 38b.

Chazal tell us that even after the sin, Adam never lost his superhuman strengths — they were just buried deep inside of him and his descendants to follow. Consequently, even today, inside every one of us these superhuman strengths can be found.

R. Shmuelevitz brings many Torah narratives where people actually achieved "the unachievable" because of these strengths.

He explains that Basya's arm did not miraculously stretch and then miraculously shrink back down to size. Rather, Basya knew how to utilize her superhuman strengths that she inherited from Adam and with them bypassed the laws of nature.

When Yaakov Avinu met Rachel for the first time, he was able to roll off that enormous rock from the well as if he was taking off a bottle cap (when it should have taken tens of people to roll it off).[73]

These events were definitely miraculous, but they were not miracles; they were just people utilizing their own superhuman strengths, which they "inherited" from Adam haRishon.

R. Shmuelevitz writes that anybody who is willing to "think big" and focus intently on his goal can channel his superhuman strengths and accomplish "the impossible." That means we all can concentrate during *davening*, host a *sheva brachos*, learn a *mishmor*, or not get upset at our friends and family if we want to. We can even finish *Shas* as well, or establish a *chessed* organization, a *neshei*[74] or even a *kollel*.[75]

Practically speaking, it is difficult to generate such energy on our own. However, external obligations can help. For example, people find the wherewithal to finish a project when they are being pressed by a deadline.

So too, by creating external obligations to motivate us, we might

73 *Bereishis* 29:10.

74 A women's group.

75 Be careful; the *yetzer hara* definitely does not mind if people utilize these strengths to walk on broken glass and break bricks, but to use them to better our spirituality is a different story. It takes time and energy to figure out how to implement this idea to one's own spiritual growth. Look in *Saam Derech*, by R. Simcha Ziskind Brody on *Parshas Vayakhel* 35:27, where he shows us how the *yetzer hara* can complicate matters and get us to use our strengths in the wrong places.

surprise ourselves as to what we could accomplish. Shabbos afternoon, for example, is a difficult time to learn. The *chulent* works like a sleeping pill and our beds call to us. To find the resources to muster up enough strength to make it to the *Beis Medrash* is far from easy. Here is the place to incorporate that obligatory *chavrusa* that could help bring one's strengths to fruition.

In conclusion, we all have inside of us superhuman strengths that we inherited from Adam haRishon. Every one of us has the means to finish *Shas*, to build that *kollel*, or to host that *sheva brachos*. Perhaps if we start on a smaller scale and utilize our external obligations, we might one day actually reach the "unreachable."

THE PINTELE YID

PARSHAS SHEMOS

וְהִנֵּה הַסְּנֶה בֹּעֵר בָּאֵשׁ וְהַסְּנֶה אֵינֶנּוּ אֻכָּל (ג, ב)

And behold, the bush was burning in a fire, and the bush was not being burned up.

Moshe Rabbeinu's first prophecy was about a bush that was being burned, but not being burned up. The Slonimer Rebbe explains that the bush symbolized the Jewish *neshamah*, and the fire that was burning it symbolized the *tumah* of Mitzrayim. Hashem was teaching Moshe that even though the *neshamos* of Klal Yisroel were "burning," sunken in the forty-nine gates of *tumah*, they were not being burned up.[76]

This prophecy was a lesson for Moshe Rabbeinu and for all eternity. Deep inside of us lies a yearning *neshamah* that can never be extinguished, because it is our essence. No matter how far we have fallen, or how engulfed we are in the impurities of the world, our *neshamah* will always yearn and live for Hashem.[77] The *seforim* call it the *pintele yid*, and for those that have tapped into it, it has become their lifeline; and

76 To say that even before the Torah was given, and before the formation of Klal Yisroel, that every Jew had that *pintele yid* seems to me like a very big *chiddush*.

77 Look in Rashi in *Sanhedrin* 76b, s.v. "*Rava.*"

for those that are still searching, it will eventually bring them close.[78]

If for some reason a Jew feels as if he has lost all of his Jewishness and *emunah*, he must know that such feelings are false, because it cannot be lost. Somehow, his *yetzer hara* has just succeeded in hiding it from him.

The truth is that even Moshe Rabbeinu thought that Klal Yisroel had lost its spark until Hashem told him otherwise. "Moshe, although it may appear to you as if Klal Yisroel's *emunah* has vanished, it hasn't. I can see deeper inside of them than you, and I can see that their *neshamos* are yearning for Me."[79]

Moshe's prophecy can bring a great deal of comfort to a person who feels as if he has lost his passion for *Yiddishkeit*. The prophecy taught us that his passion might be hidden from him, but it has not gone. It just needs to be rediscovered, and once it is rediscovered, it will take him to the highest of heights. The *pintele yid* inside every one of us is a storehouse of yearning for Hashem just waiting to be unleashed.

The lesson of the Burning Bush is eternal. Anyone who is honest with himself can find the want and desire to do the right thing and serve Hashem with all of his heart. Let us rediscover our spark and let it carry us for the rest of our lives.[80]

---

78 The *Nesivos Shalom* compares it to the *Koach haYuli*, as explained in the Ramban in *Parshas Bereishis*.

79 The *Nesivos Shalom* brings the *Medrash Rabbah* 3:3. The *pasuk* seems to be repetitive. It is written: *"Raei ra'esee es ani ami,"* mentioning the word *Raei*, which means "to see" twice, inferring a double vision.

80 *Nesivos Shalom*, vol. 2, pg. 257, *"Kei be'chipazon yatzasa m'eretz Mitzrayim."*

DON'T FORGET THE BASICS

PARSHAS VAEIRA

לְמַעַן תֵּדַע כִּי אֲנִי יְהֹוָה בְּקֶרֶב הָאָרֶץ (ח, יח)
In order that you should know that I am Hashem.

Mr. Hart stood up at his son's *sheva brachos* and started to speak. "I would like you all to know that Hashem did not help me marry off my son." The room became silent and Mr. Hart continued. "The word 'help' implies that I did the majority of the work and Hashem helped me put it all together. To say such a thing would be a heresy. Hashem did not help me because He did everything. Just as Hashem split the sea, He married off my son."

R. Shlomo Volbe once came to R. Yechezkel (Chatzkel) Levenstein, the late Mirrer *mashgiach*, for advice concerning one of his *talmidim*. When parting, R. Chatzkel turned to R. Volbe and told him that a *mashgiach's* job is to ingrain into his *talmidim* an *emunah* in the *Ribono Shel Olam.*

The Gateshead Rov, R. Betzalel Rakov, also visited R. Chatzkel, and after he told him that he was a *maggid shiur*, R. Chatzkel told him that the job of a *maggid shiur* is to ingrain into his *talmidim* an *emunah* in the *Ribono Shel Olam.*

An executive once came to R. Chatzkel for advice on a family matter. After hearing that he was a workingman, R. Chetzkel also told him that the job of a *baal habos* is to ingrain into his family an *emunah* in the *Ribono Shel Olam*.[81]

R. Chazkel was not referring to Jews who were ignorant of their Judaism. He was referring to the many Jews who go through their lives performing mitzvos and studying Torah without truly feeling in their hearts that the world has a Creator. R. Chatzkel taught these influential figures the severity of this fundamental feeling and that it needs constant *chizuk*.

The *Eser Makkos, Yetzias Mitzrayim* and *Kerias Yam Suf* screamed this very fact to the world some 3,300 years ago, and its message still rings today. *Yetzias Mitzrayim* is mentioned no less than fifty times in the Torah and has tens of mitzvos associated with it because it is so elementary to our *Yiddishkeit*.

However, such a fundamental idea can quickly be forgotten.

Whether we are trying to find the right yeshiva, seminary, *shidduch*, or *chavrusa*, or we need help in our business, we must constantly remind ourselves that the world has a Creator who loves us and is taking care of us. As humorous as it may sound, these *parshiyos* can remind us of how vital Hashem is to our everyday lives.

---

81 I heard this from R. Asher Zelig Rubenstein, the late Rosh Yeshiva of Toras Simcha in Yerushalayim.

ARE YOU IN CONTROL OF THE SITUATION OR IS IT IN CONTROL OF YOU?

PARSHAS VAEIRA

כִּי בַּפַּעַם הַזֹּאת אֲנִי שֹׁלֵחַ... אֶל לִבְּךָ וּבַעֲבָדֶיךָ וּבְעַמֶּךָ (ט, יד)

For this time I shall send all My plagues ...against your heart, and upon your servants and your people.

As the Egged bus started to pull away from its stop, a terrible screech came from its rear doors. A mother was getting onto the bus with her baby stroller as the bus doors closed. The stroller had toppled over, the mother was knocked off the bus and the bus came to an immediate halt. While the surrounding passengers picked up the stroller and the mother picked up her screaming baby and managed to calm him down, the passengers in the front of the bus jumped from their seats to yell at the driver.

To my amazement, the driver just sat there listening to the hurricane of criticism until it finally subsided. (You can only have a yelling match if there are two people yelling at each other). The driver calmly got up from his seat, walked to the back of the bus, stood up in front of the mother, and asked her for forgiveness in front of everybody.

A natural reaction when being screamed and yelled at is to scream and yell back louder. However, this driver did not do that. He chose to walk in Hashem's ways and reacted with patience and respect.

The *Me'am Loez* writes that Hashem wanted to teach us how to use our attribute of patience in place of anger in this week's *parshah*.[82] Even though the *Mitzrim* deserved to die after treating Hashem's children so harshly, nonetheless Hashem withheld His anger at first and killed the *Mitzrim*'s animals before He killed them. "Learn from me," said Hashem, "and do not react out of anger when somebody upsets you. Be in control of your anger and don't let your anger be in control of you."[83]

As I gazed at this bus driver, I could not help but see a beautiful person. That day I discovered that real beauty is more than skin deep. It must be when our internal Godliness shines out.[84]

---

82 *Me'am Loez*, in the name of the *Bina L'etim*, ch. 15.

83 Look in *Chovos Halevavos, Sha'ar Hakenia*, ch. 1.

84 Look in *Sifsei Chaim, Moadim*, vol. 2, Chanukah — *Tikkun Hoed*.

THE THREE THOUSAND SIX HUNDRED AND SEVENTY FIVE DOLLAR MIRACLE

PARSHAS BO

לְמַעַן תֵּדְעוּן אֲשֶׁר יַפְלֶה יְהֹוָה בֵּין מִצְרַיִם וּבֵין יִשְׂרָאֵל (יא, ז)

So that you will know that Hashem will have differentiated between Mitzrayim and Yisroel.

My wife and I lived in Zichron Yaakov (a small town just south of Haifa) for the first year and a half of our marriage, after which we moved to Yerushalayim. Moving to Yerushalayim was like moving into the big leagues. Aside for the hustle and bustle of the city, our rent was going to jump from two hundred dollars a month, which we barely managed, to six hundred a month. In addition, our future landlord wanted six months rent up front! How in the world were we going to come up with three thousand and six hundred dollars with a *kollel* stipend of two hundred and fifty dollars a month?

We decided to borrow the money from a *gemach* and pay it back in installments. As I walked down the stairs of our apartment to the *gemach*, a Federal Express truck pulled into our small street looking for me. The deliveryman handed me an envelope with a check totaling three thousand, six hundred and seventy-five dollars! It was just enough money to cover the six months rent and the check-cashing fees. Now that was *hashgachah pratis*.

In truth, *hashgachah pratis* goes far beyond the daily "mini-miracles" that we encounter. It is one of the most fundamental components in our *emunah*,[85] and it is the basis of the entire Torah![86] *Hashgachah pratis* means that there is no such thing as coincidence or happenstance. Everything that happens, even events that appear as bad, are intrinsically good and only happen because Hashem wants them to happen. Moreover, it means that Hashem is guiding and directing the entire universe for our benefit.

This became apparent to the world during the *Eser Makkos*. Already by *makkas Dam*, Hashem was saving the Jews and not the *Mitzrim*.[87] All the *Eser Makkos* and *Yetzias Mitzrayim* have become our *binyan av* (prototype) for this timeless lesson.[88]

R. Yechezkel Levenstein writes that people who live with *hashgachah pratis* live a life of peace and tranquility.[89] They understand that all their experiences and events have all been tailor-made by Hashem. By standing firm in their beliefs, they find comfort and even joy during the grimmest of situations.

However, to live with *hashgachah pratis* is not an easy task and takes a lifetime of toil to internalize. Aside from drawing encouragement from these *parshios*, my wife and I have acquired for ourselves a three thousand, six hundred and seventy-five dollar miracle as our *binyan av* that constantly reminds us that Hashem is with us every

---

85 Look at the first of the Rambam's thirteen *ikkarim* and in the *Sefer haIkkarim* 1:4, s.v. *"Haderech haNachon."*

86 Look in the Ramban at the end of *Parshas Bo*, s.v. *"u'min hanisim"* and the *Orchos Chaim la'Rosh* 26.

87 If a Jew and a *Mitzri* were drinking from the very same cup, the *Mitzri* would have drunken blood, and the Jew water.

88 Ramban at the end of *Parshas Bo*.

89 His commentary on the *Orchos Chaim la'Rosh*, ibid., s.v. *"Rabbeinu."*

single step of the way. I am sure that you too have your own personal "mini-miracles" to give you direction and light along your way to a life filled with *hashgachah pratis*.

DON'T BE LIKE AN ELEPHANT

PARSHAS BESHALACH

הִתְיַצְּבוּ וּרְאוּ אֶת יְשׁוּעַת ה' (יד, יג)
Stand fast and see the salvation of Hashem.

Many circuses tie their baby elephants to a peg immediately after birth to prevent them from running away. Astonishing as it may sound, this little peg prevents them from running away even when they are fully grown! Their unsuccessful attempts of trying to pull out the peg as a baby convince them that they will never succeed in pulling it out. Consequently, they remain confined to that very same peg even when they are fully grown!

Klal Yisroel feared for their lives at the sea. The Torah tells us that they were afraid of Pharaoh's six hundred chariots that were chasing after them. The Ibn Ezra does not understand the logic behind their fears. If Klal Yisroel had six hundred thousand armed men,[90] why couldn't they wipe out Pharaoh's six hundred chariots with ease?

The Ibn Ezra explains that after living for over a century in dread

90 *Rashi* on *Shemos* 13:18.

of their Egyptian taskmasters, there was no way that Klal Yisroel could now turn around and fight against them. Those years of dread blinded them from seeing how enormous they had become, and conditioned them for life. They perceived themselves as the weak and feeble slaves without any self-worth and the *Mitzrim* as the mighty oppressors. True, there was a ratio of a thousand Jewish men to every *Mitzri*, but those years of conditioning already formulated a new reality, and that new reality caused them to react with fear.

That new reality also led them to believe that they lacked the inner strength needed to wage war against Canaan and eventually take over Eretz Yisroel. That is why Hashem let that generation die in the wilderness and waited to lead the next generation into Eretz Yisroel, a generation that was conditioned with the Clouds of Glory together with constant miracles. Such conditioning gave them a true sense of self-worth, character, and fortitude that enabled them to fight the *Canaanim* and eventually take over Eretz Yisroel.

Even today, life's challenges and experiences play a role in how we perceive ourselves. How many thousands of people in our generation suffer from the poison called "I can't"? Perhaps they tried to *daven* with the correct *kavanah*, learn a *daf* of Gemara, or do an act of *chessed* and did not succeed. As a result, they mistakenly concluded that they are underachievers and failures simply because they tried once and failed.

Instead of understanding that all these things take years of investment and a certain level of maturity, they allowed the experience to paint an erroneous self-image of themselves, which became unshakeable to them even later on in their lives. Such people usually find their underachievement too painful to face, and instead of turning inward to fix themselves, they choose to turn outward by seeking new and easier avenues of life, believing that the initial ones were not for them. Perhaps we could say that such people are their own worst enemy.

Nachson ben Aminadav leaped into the sea because he succeeded in seeing past his self-imposed limitations. The Medrash explains that Nachshon learned this from Basya's outstretched arm.[91] Although Nachshon viewed himself with limited capabilities, he reminded himself of Basya, for she too was limited and yet rose above her limitations and reached the "unreachable."[92] He understood that all people, including himself, have enormous superhuman strengths that are just waiting to be unleashed. He succeeded in actualizing his strengths, and the rest is history.

Some people are able to rise above their self-imposed limitations by themselves; others need external help.

What is important to remember is that no matter how we perceive ourselves, we are in truth a million times greater and mightier than whatever we could have imagined.

---

91 I only heard the *Medrash*. The *Medrash* is coming to explain the *pasuk*: "*V'yar Yisroel es ha-yad ha-gedolah* — And Yisroel saw the big hand."

92 See above, on *Parshas Shemos*.

APPRECIATING CRITICISM

PARSHAS YISRO

וַיִּשְׁמַע מֹשֶׁה לְקוֹל חֹתְנוֹ (יח, כד)

Moshe listened to the voice of his father-in-law [Yisro].

How was the great Moshe Rabbeinu, leader of Klal Yisroel and father of all the prophets, able to accept Yisro's criticism? Nobody enjoys hearing his or her faults and weaknesses. Why wasn't he embarrassed or personally offended by Yisro's words? "Moshe, what you are doing is not good. You're going to wear yourself out, along with the rest of the nation. Your responsibility is too great. You can't do it alone!"[93]

Moshe's willingness to accept Yisro's advice may be surprising, but it does not surpass Chazal's expectations of every Jew. Chazal taught us to accept criticism and even to love it![94] The Rosh takes this a step further and obligates us to rejoice when hearing rebuke, just as a person rejoices when finding a treasure.[95]

Perhaps with a bit of background, we too can reach such levels. Let us try to understand what Chazal is teaching us.

Society has convinced itself that flaws are a sign of inadequacy and

---

93 *Shemos* 18:13–27.

94 *Avos* 6:6.

95 *Orchos Chaim la'Rosh* 45.

failure. This has forced people to perform on a much higher level than they are really on. People must be perfect even before they have perfected themselves. In addition, one must continuously, consciously or subconsciously, cover up one's faults and weaknesses in order to portray the image of "the perfect human being."

For a person who was brought up in this worldview, criticism is not only counterproductive, it is also difficult to accept because it reveals what is supposed to be hidden.

It is true that we are supposed to aspire towards self-perfection, however to say or assume that we have reached our perfection is far from the truth. The Chasam Sofer explains the words "*Boreh nefashos rabos ve'chesronan*" as "Hashem created everything with its deficiencies, shortcomings, and faults."[96] We, too, were born with our own set of them, and our job in this world is to try to rectify them.[97] Such a task does not happen overnight, or over a few years, but is a lifelong goal.

When a person understands that self-perfection is only a goal and not a reality, he can appreciate criticism and even welcome it. He can view criticism as a helpful tool in his quest for self-perfection. Of course, it is far more pleasant when someone corrects us tactfully, but since our goal is self-perfection, we can appreciate the criticism, even if it is offered less than ideally.

Why is criticism a prerequisite for growth? Aside from the fact that we were not born knowing everything,[98] we are also biased towards ourselves. We tend to view ourselves as "all-around good people," with a thousand and one reasons and rationalizations to justify our actions. This blinds us from seeing the aspects of ourselves that we have not perfected and that still need addressing. Only an outsider can show us these points. In fact, many Torah giants like the Vilna Gaon and the Maharshal had "professional rebukers" who aided them in their quest for self-perfection.

This approach to criticism can help us understand how being cen-

---

96 *Toras Moshe, Parshas Eikev*.

97 Look in the beginning of *Even Shlomo*.

98 *Mesilas Yesharim* 12.

sured can be compared to finding a treasure. Rebuke, when viewed in a fresh light, is vital direction along the road towards self-perfection. Criticism is priceless, because without it one's goal can be lost forever.

The following story illustrates this point: When the Sefas Emes was a young boy, he would study immediately after *davening* with his *chavrusa* until eleven in the morning. Afterwards, he attended a private *shiur* by his *zeide*, the Chiddushei haRim. One day he and his *chavrusa* lost track of the time and he arrived at eleven-thirty instead of eleven o'clock. As soon as he entered the room, the Chiddushei haRim rebuked his grandson. "Leibel, what's going to become of you? All you're doing is wasting your time playing games with your friends."

The Sefas Emes stood in absolute silence. Later, his *chavrusa* asked him why he did not explain that they had lost track of time because they were so engrossed in their learning. Leibel answered, "How often does a person get the opportunity to hear criticism from a Torah giant like my *zeide*? To dismiss such rebuke is a golden opportunity lost."

Now we can understand how Moshe accepted Yisro's criticism and implemented it right away. In like fashion, our reaction to criticism depends on our outlook. Either we can feel hurt, embarrassed, and insulted, or we can feel grateful and fortunate for receiving direction in our quest for self-improvement and self-perfection.

THE JEWISH SLAVE: A WINDOW INTO THE BEAUTY OF THE TORAH

PARSHAS MISHPATIM

כִּי תִקְנֶה עֶבֶד עִבְרִי (כא, ב)

When you will buy a Hebrew servant.

Handling thieves is not an easy task. Today the courts imprison them, but imprisonment has its setbacks too. Beyond the resentment and animosity that thieves amass during their sentence, they learn from their cellmates how to become better thieves and sink further into crime. When they are finally released, their old debts, and the newly accumulated ones that their families have built up while they were in prison, haunt them endlessly. This makes it virtually impossible for them to start anew. As a result, they fall back into their old habits and begin stealing, even better than before, thanks to the new tricks that they learned while in prison.

The Torah, on the other hand, has a completely different approach. The Torah requires that a thief who cannot pay back his debts be sold into slavery. This enables the thief to raise enough money to pay off his previous debts and begin anew. The Torah also dictates that his master support the thief's family while he is a slave, which in turn prevents new debts from accumulating. When he is finally freed, the Torah extends its mercy once again and obligates his master to send him off with a substantial sum of money. Perhaps one of the underlying reasons for this mitzvah is to help him get back onto his feet.

In addition to helping him monetarily, the Torah also attempts to rehabilitate him ethically. Criminals were not born criminals. They are usually a product of their environment and/or upbringing. Maybe they were orphans or came from a poor family, which gave them a very low self-image. As a result, they found themselves trying to "make a living" and fending for themselves. Nobody taught them how to live, how to blend into society, and how to be a decent human being.

However, once this thief will be sold as a slave, he will discover a new world. He will see how his "new family" will treat him with the utmost respect and dignity. He will eat the same quality of food as them, if not better. If there is only one pillow in the house, he is the one to receive it!

Moreover, the thief will be sold to a home filled with Torah and *yiras Shamayim*, thus imbuing him with *derech eretz* and *middos tovos*.[99] He will learn how to be a *mentsch*, what it means to have respect for one another, and a feeling of self-worth. He will learn what a beautiful Shabbos table is, how to interact with people as *bnei Torah* should, and that a home is built on love and *shalom bayis*.

After living in such an environment for a total of six years, he will hopefully have a different impression of himself along with the rest of society. He will have no previous debts haunting him or his family, and will have a substantial amount of money to start a business in order to begin anew. More importantly, he will have accumulated Torah ethics and a feeling of self-worth. He might actually begin to think, "Hey, how can I go out and steal from the world? Not only

99 Look in *Lev Shalom* by R. Sholom Shwadron.

do I have dignity and self-worth, but I even have the means at my disposal to open a business!" The Ibn Ezra explains the reason why the master sends him off with gifts is to give him that boost of self-esteem and self-worth that is very much needed.[100]

Just as a worried and concerned father tries to save his son from crime, Hashem created the *parshah* of "the Jewish slave" as an avenue of return for His son who has strayed. The wayward child is such a priority to Hashem that He put it first on the list of all the *dinim* of the *parshah*.

The *halachos* of the Jewish slave are just a small glimpse into the wisdom of the Torah and its perfection. It is not only a "rule book"; it is a "manual for life." Just as the Torah's plan for a thief is an ingenious one, so too everything else. The Torah has the power to bring happiness, joy, and meaning to every Jewish person. It is the most precious thing in the world.[101]

So many people are searching for direction in their lives, searching for truth and stability, and are left empty-handed. We were given the gift of life at Har Sinai and when we open our hearts to its wisdom, we will find solutions for every situation that we will ever encounter.

We may forget from time to time how precious and special the Torah is. Even a bag of priceless diamonds can get annoying and bothersome in one's pocket after some time, that is, if he forgets their true value. Let us use this *parshah* of the "Jewish slave" to remind ourselves of the wonderful diamond that we are carrying. Let us learn to cherish it and allow it to guide our lives in every way possible.

---

100 Look in *Ibn Ezra* on *Devorim* 15:14.

101 Based on *Darchei Mussar*.

TWO PENSION PLANS

PARSHAS TERUMAH

וְיִקְחוּ לִי תְּרוּמָה (כה, ב)
They should take for me a portion.

Baron Rothschild handed his children two letters before he passed away. He instructed them to open one immediately upon his death, and the second a month later. When they opened the first letter, they found the following message written inside: "My last request is that I should be buried wearing my socks." Even though his children were perplexed by such a request, they still tried to honor it. However, the *rabbonim* prohibited them from doing so and he was buried without his socks.

After the month had passed, his children anxiously opened up the second letter to discover another message: "I know that you did not bury me wearing my socks as I had requested, since it is against halachah. You are probably wondering why, then, did I request it in the first place. My answer is to teach you, my dear children, this eternal lesson: A person cannot even take his socks with him to the next world. Only his Torah and mitzvos will accompany him."

The commentaries at the beginning of our *parshah* ask why when Hashem told Klal Yisroel to contribute to the *Mishkan,* He told them to "take" their contribution — *"Vayikchu li terumah"* — and not "give" it. People do not take their own contributions, they give them!

The Beis Halevi explains that when Klal Yisroel contributed to the *Mishkan,* they were actually taking for themselves. He reminds us that our acquisitions, wealth, and even talents that we have are not ours.[102] Hashem has "lent" them to us for the performance of Torah and mitzvos. However, when we do use them for the right reasons, Hashem gives them to us for all eternity.

That is why the Torah uses the term taking instead of giving when referring to contributing towards the *Mishkan*. Hashem is teaching us how to "take" for ourselves. When we utilize our tools for *tzedakah, ruchnius,* and *avodas Hashem,* we are in essence transferring them directly into our spiritual bank account in the World to Come, where they will be ours for eternity. Hence, when Klal Yisroel gave to the *Mishkan*, they were in essence taking for themselves.

King Monbaz was overly generous when it came to giving *tzedakah* during the years of famine. His family approached him and inquired, "Your ancestors saved up for many years, and now you are giving it all away?" He answered them by saying, "On the contrary, my brethren, the Torah teaches us that the *tzedakah* that you give will eventually be yours.[103] Therefore, I am the one that is saving and not them!"[104]

How can King Monbaz say that he was saving for himself when in actuality he was giving his wealth away? The answer is that when a person gives his money away to *tzedakah* or contributes it to one of Hashem's causes, he is in essence transferring it into his spiritual bank account and thus keeping it for himself forever.

Besides our regular pension plan, we must remember and consider our other pension plan, which will be paid out in the next world. Nothing of this world will accompany us there, not even a pair of socks; nothing except for our *tzedakah*, Torah, and mitzvos. Every time we give correctly, we are in essence taking for ourselves by investing in our other pension plan for all of eternity.

---

102 Look in *Ahavas Chessed* 3:4.

103 *Devorim* 24: *"A'lecha te'heye tzedakah."*

104 *Bava Basra* 11a.

KLAL YISROEL IS FOR HASHEM

THE TZITZ

PARSHAS TETZAVEH

וְהָיָה עַל מִצְחוֹ תָּמִיד לְרָצוֹן לָהֶם לִפְנֵי ה׳ (כח, לו–לח)

And it shall be on his head always, to bring them favor before Hashem.

It was *erev* Pesach in Berditchev and R. Levi Yitzchok asked his *shamash* to bring him some Turkish furs, tobacco, and liquor. His *shamash* questioned the *rebbe:* "But Rebbe, we are at war with the Turks, and the Czar has banned all Turkish products. The products that the Rebbe has requested are nowhere to be found." "I understand your dilemma," said R. Levi Yitzchok, "but you must search for them nonetheless."

Two hours later, the home of R. Levi Yitzchok was filled with tens, if not hundreds, of Turkish furs, tobacco, and liquor. R. Levi Yitzchok turned to his *shamash* and said, "Now I want you to bring me a piece of *chometz.*" The *shamash* wondered out loud, "But Rebbe, it is *erev Pesach!*" R. Levi Yitzchok replied, "Please, just do as I have requested."

After six hours of searching, the *shamash* came back empty-handed. Not even a morsel of *chometz* was found. R. Levi Yitzchok turned to the heavens with a big smile and said, "Dear Father in Heaven, see how much Klal Yisroel loves You. The Czar made a law that no Turkish products can enter Russia, he hired a police force to enforce the law and yet we can still find them in almost every home! However, You Hashem told Klal Yisroel over three-thousand years ago that they could not have any *chometz* for the whole week of *Pesach*. Even though, there are no police to enforce Your laws, we cannot find a morsel of bread in the whole town of Berditchev. Hashem, Klal Yisroel loves you and loves to keep your mitzvos!"

The *Tzitz* was one of the eight garments that the *Kohen Gadol* wore while serving in the Beis Hamikdash. Aside for the honor and splendor that it brought him, it did a tremendous service for Klal Yisroel. The *Tzitz* was able to arouse Hashem's attribute of love. Once Hashem's attribute of love was aroused, He accepted an invalid *korban* as if it was perfectly valid![105,106]

What was the *Tzitz's* secret? How did it arouse this attribute of love and thus gain favor in Hashem's eyes?

The *Ohr Hachaim haKadosh* reveals the secret.[107] The *Tzitz* had two words engraved onto it: *Kadosh La'Hashem* (Holy to Hashem). He explains that the word *Kadosh* (Holy) alludes to Klal Yisroel and the word *La'Hashem* means, "is for Hashem." Hence, "Klal Yisroel is for Hashem" was engraved on the *Tzitz*. This implied that Klal Yisroel is only and entirely for Hashem. The *Ohr Hachaim* understands that this alludes to Klal Yisroel's inner desire to be completely connected,

---

105 A *korban* that was invalidated because of *tumah* (impure) would be accepted as if it was a *tahor* (pure) *korban*.

106 The Rambam writes that a *Kohen* is not permitted to sprinkle the blood of a *tamei korban* onto the *Mizbe'ach*, and even if he did, the *korban* is invalid. However, if for some reason he sprinkled the blood while the *Kohen Gadol* was wearing the holy *tzitz*, the *korban* would then be favorable in Hashem's eyes and Hashem would accept it as if it was *tahor*. Look in *Yuma* 7a; Rambam, *pesulei ha'mukdashim* 1:34.

107 Based on the *Ohr Hachaim* on *Shemos* 28:38.

subservient, and devoted to Hashem. So every time the *Kohen Gadol* wore the *Tzitz*, it in essence proclaimed this powerful message and awakened Hashem's attribute of love.

Once Hashem saw that "we are to our beloved,"[108] Hashem in turn reciprocated with "and my beloved is to me,"[109] — "I love you too." One of the ways that Hashem expressed this love was by accepting favorably an invalid *korban* as if it was valid.

The powerful message that the *Tzitz* proclaimed still exists in every one of us. Every Jew's inner desire is to be completely connected, subservient and devoted to Hashem. Every Jewish soul yearns for closeness to Hashem and wants to make Hashem his beloved. Rashi adds that every Jewish soul thirsts for fear of Hashem and desires to fulfill His mitzvos.[110] If for some reason, we find ourselves not living with this thirst, it is only because our *yetzer hara* succeeded in hiding it from us.[111]

We can learn from the *Tzitz* that we do not have to create love and devotion to Hashem and His mitzvos because they are part of our essence. We just have to uncover them and bring them out to fruition.[112] In addition, the *Tzitz* reminds us of the precious relationship that we have with Hashem. As much as we make Hashem our beloved, He will reciprocate with "and my beloved is to me" and show us His love.

---

108 *Ani Ledodi...*

109 *V'dodi li.*

110 Look in Rashi in *Sanhedrin* 76b, s.v. "*Rava.*"

111 *Brachos* 17b: "*Ribono Shel Olam*...our will is to do Your will. What is stopping us? The *sa'or she'b'esa.*"

112 See above, on *Parshas Shemos*, "*The Pintele Yid.*"

THE BROKEN ENGAGEMENT

PARSHAS KI SISA

כִּי אוֹת הִוא בֵּינִי וּבֵינֵיכֶם (לא, יג)
It is a sign between Me and you.

A dreadful thing happened in a town just outside of Radin. One of the Jewish merchants started to keep his store open on Shabbos. The *rabbonim* of the town, along with the townspeople, tried to talk to him, but he refused to listen to reason. One day the Chafetz Chaim visited the town and decided to go and speak to the merchant. Others tried to dissuade him, out of fear that the merchant would treat him disrespectfully, but the Chafetz Chaim refused to be dissuaded.

He took the merchant's hand in his own, held it tightly, and started to cry. As the tears rolled down his cheeks, he whispered, "*Shabbos kodesh, Shabbos kodesh,*" repeatedly. This continued for a few minutes until the Chafetz Chaim finally left.

The next Shabbos the store was closed.

Hashem gave us a gift called Shabbos. It symbolizes the special relationship that we have with Hashem and our preciousness to Him. The Chafetz Chaim compares Shabbos to the gifts that a *chasan* gives his *kallah*. Just as a *chasan* expresses his love to his *kallah* with gifts, so too Hashem expresses His love to us with the gift of Shabbos.[113] The more we honor the Shabbos, the more we demonstrate that we cherish that relationship.

The Chafetz Chaim takes this analogy one step further. If a *chasan* and *kallah* have not seen each other for an extended period, people start to wonder if the engagement is still on. However, once they see that the *kallah* still has the *chasan*'s gifts, they are reassured that everything is all right. However, if the *kallah* returns the gifts, it is clear that the engagement was broken.

Says the Chafetz Chaim, if a Jew, *chas v'shalom*, returns the "gift of Shabbos" to Hashem, he has indicated that he no longer wants the relationship.

The aforementioned story is usually told to demonstrate the Chafetz Chaim's unique method of censure. However, after hearing the Chafetz Chaim's analogy of the *chasan* and *kallah*, we can understand it in a new light. The Chafetz Chaim was crying over a broken engagement.

When a Jew keeps Shabbos properly, he not only demonstrates that he desires his relationship with Hashem, but that he cherishes it as well.

113 *Chafetz Chaim on the Torah* 31:12.

GOLDEN OPPORTUNITIES

PARSHAS KI SISA

מִי לַה' אֵלָי (לב, כו)

Whoever is for Hashem, let him come to me.

When R. Shimon Schwab was a young boy, he had an experience that changed his life.[114] He was fortunate to spend a Shabbos with the great Chafetz Chaim.

The Chafetz Chaim asked him during that Shabbos if he knew that he was a *Kohen* and R. Schwab told him yes. He then asked, "Maybe you are a *Kohen* as well?" "No, I am not. "A Levi?" R. Schwab again answered, "No." "How unfortunate," replied the Chafetz Chaim.

Then the Chafetz Chaim went on to explain what he meant. "When the Beis Hamikdash will be rebuilt, every Jew will have a burning desire to participate in the *avodah*.[115] However, not everybody will have that privilege and I want to tell you why. About three thousand years ago, after the *Chet haEgel*, Moshe called out *"Mi l'Hashem ay'lie"* — "Whoever is for Hashem, let him come [and join] me!" My *zaidie* stepped forward to show his loyalty to Hashem and your *zaidie* did not. Hashem rewarded my *zaidie* for this act by giving him and his

114 Brought in *Ma'yan Bais Hashoava* 32:26. This experience took place in the year 5690.

115 The service in the Beis Hamikdash.

ancestors an eternal gift, the *zechus* to serve in the Beis Hamikdash. That is why I will have the *zechus* to participate while you, unfortunately, will not."

The Chafetz Chaim concluded, "Shimon, you are probably wondering why I am telling you this. The answer is, that we all have moments in our lives where we will hear that inner call of: "*Mi la'Hashem ay'lie*." Shimon, when you hear it, run after it with all your might and don't lose out like your *zaidie* did."

Together with that big "whoever is for Hashem, let him come [and join] me!" are silent calls that come up every day. Every time we overcome our *yetzer hara*, every time we break our *middos*, every time we go to a daily *shiur* when we are "too tired" to attend, we are actively showing our loyalty and devotion to Hashem. In truth, this can prepare us for the big *"Mi la'Hashem ay'lie"* that we may encounter one day.

This is what the Chafetz Chaim told R. Schwab before he left to America. "Get yourself ready to run with all your might to aid Klal Yisroel when the time demands," and such he did.

Parenthetically, just a few *parshios* ago,[116] the *Ohr Hachaim haKadosh* taught us that the more someone shows his loyalty and devotion to Hashem, the more Hashem's attribute of love is aroused and the more Hashem will show His love in return. When *shevet Levi* showed their loyalty and devotion, Hashem's attribute of love was aroused. Hashem reciprocated by showering them with the everlasting gift of being able to serve in the Beis Hamikdash.

We can learn from here how golden just one act of devotion to Hashem is. Such an act creates rippling effects for all eternity. Let us take the lesson and show our loyalty and devotion to Hashem, just as the Chafetz Chaim's *zaidie* did.

116 *Parshas Tetzaveh, Shemos* 28:38.

A DAY OF PEACE AND TRANQUILITY

PARSHAS VAYAKHEL

שֵׁשֶׁת יָמִים תֵּעָשֶׂה מְלָאכָה (לה, ב)
For six days work will be done.

Mr. Hartman was one of the few builders in Eretz Yisroel some sixty years ago. He was anxiously awaiting an extremely large and expensive overseas shipment of cement to arrive so he could begin his new project. (Sixty years ago, cement had to be imported and was very expensive). He was notified on *erev* Shabbos that the shipment finally arrived and was ready to be picked up at the port of Yaffo.

His workers told him that there was a big rainstorm coming in on Shabbos and if he would not pick up the shipment today, it will all be ruined. However, it was too close to Shabbos for him to do anything. He would never desecrate Shabbos for all the money in the world and left his cement at the port for the whole Shabbos. As the rain poured down on Shabbos, Mr. Hartman rested, learned, *davened* and enjoyed the Shabbos — "his day of rest."

When he finally got to the port on *motzei Shabbos,* he could not believe his eyes. Somebody had covered all of his cement and not a single bag was ruined! He found out later that another building company also received a large shipment of cement that very same day and sent workers to cover up their shipment on Shabbos and "by mistake" they covered Mr. Hartman's cement instead! The builders that were *mechalel Shabbos* lost their cement, while Mr. Hartman's cement was saved.

The Torah says, "For six days, work will be done... (תֵּעָשֶׂה)", and not "You should do work (תַּעֲשֶׂה) for six days..."

The author of the *Kitzur Shulchan Aruch*, R. Shlomo Ganzfried writes that serenity on Shabbos comes from the correct mindset.[117] One has to know and believe that his hard work does not make the *parnasah*;[118] rather it comes from Hashem putting the *brachah* and *hatzlacha* into his hard work. The Torah writes "work will be done" (passively) to remind us that we do not make the money,[119] rather the money is made "by itself" with Hashem's *brachah*.[120]

With such a mindset, one can let go of his workload and enjoy the peace and tranquility found in Shabbos. However, a person who thinks that his *hatzlachah* stems from his own hard work and that he himself is making the money is depriving himself of that peace and tranquility. He cannot "let go" of his workload because he views Shabbos, "the day of rest," as a day of missed opportunity.

Eating fish on Shabbos reminds us of this fundamental idea. It is not our efforts that bring the success — it is Hashem's brachah. Many large fish sustain themselves by chasing after smaller fish and then swallowing them. Logic dictates that the smaller fish should be swallowed tail first. However, amazing as it may sound, when the larger fish are cut open, the smaller ones are actually facing the other direction, with their heads in first, almost as if they "accidentally" swam into the mouth of the larger fish! In hindsight, we see that it

---

117 The *Apirion*, which is brought in *Lekach Tov*. *Darchei Mussar* writes the same idea.

118 Livelihood.

119 If the Torah wanted to write "you shall work...", it should have written תַּעֲשֶׂה.

120 Look in Rashi and in the *Gur Aryeh* in *Parshas Terumah* 25:31. In fact, all of our success stems from the *brachah* and *hatzlachah* that Hashem puts into it.

was not their efforts that brought them their prey; it was Hashem placing the smaller fish into their mouths that did.

We eat fish on Shabbos to remind us that no matter how much effort one puts into his *parnasah*, we have to remember that Hashem's *brachah* feeds us (תֵּעָשֶׂה) and not our hard work (תַּעֲשֶׂה). Only with such a mindset will a person truly merit the peace and tranquility that comes with Shabbos.[121]

121 This essay was taken from *Otzeros Hatorah*, courtesy of the author HaRav Eliyahu Chaim Cohen *shlita*.

STEPPING UP TO THE PLATE

PARSHAS VAYAKHEL

וַיַּעַשׂ בְּצַלְאֵל אֶת הָאָרֹן (לז, א)
Bezalel made the Aron.

R. Nissim Yagen would regularly arrange and host *shabbatons* for secular Israelis in his own special way.[122] Towards the end of a *shabboton* he would stand up on a stage in front of over two hundred secular Israelis and, for a lack of better terms, would auction off sets of *shas* in exchange for televisions.[123] It was a sight to see. A gigantic *talmid chochom* playing the role of an auctioneer of televisions! When asked why he was doing such a crazy thing, he replied, "Because nobody else is."

R. Yagen was a man that saw the *kiyum*[124] of Klal Yisroel and Torah as his own personal responsibility and acted accordingly. Perhaps he

---

122 R. Yagen was a *talmid* of R. Aharon Kotler and the Rosh Yeshiva of Yeshivas Kehilas Yaakov in Yerushalayim.

123 When asked how he was able to afford all the Gemaras, he said that on *motzaei* Shabbos he would hire a truck and gather all the televisions, drive to the local Arab village and sell them. He would then buy Gemaras with the money and deliver them to the selected "winners" of the auction.

124 Existence.

inherited this trait from his *rebbi*, R. Aharon Kotler, who epitomized responsibly when it came to the *kiyum* of Torah in America in the early forties.

In our *parshah,* the Torah attributes the making of the *Aron ha-Kodesh* solely to Betzlel. R. Baruch Sorotzkin explains that although all of Klal Yisroel participated in making the *Aron haKodesh,*[125] the Torah writes that Betzalel made it because he made it his responsibility. Since the *Aron* is symbolic of the Torah, it is as if the Torah is saying that Betzalel was held responsible for the existence of the Torah!

R. Sorotzkin explains that when it comes to *kiyum haTorah* — keeping the Torah going, we are all equally responsible. Nobody is permitted to rely on others to get the job done.

Today's world seems to run away from responsibility. However, our *parshah* teaches us what a beautiful attribute it is and how vital it is when it comes to the existence of Torah.

After a dear friend of mine noticed the financial burden that *yom tov* expenses placed upon certain *kollel* families, he decided to raise money to help them. As of today, he raises up to six thousand dollars yearly. Nobody asked him to do it, neither did he assume that somebody else would; he just knew that it needed to be done and did it. He took the responsibility for the *kiyum* of Torah into his hands and the rest is history.

There was once a small town with only ten Jews. Every day they would all show up for *minyan*, since they knew that they were all needed for the *minyan*. It went like this for many years until one day an eleventh Jew moved into the town. The next day, only one person showed up to the *minyan* — the newcomer.

Being responsible is very commendable in the eyes of the Torah. Hashem should give us all the desire to attain such a beautiful attribute.

---

125 *Shemos Rabbah* 34:3. Hashem commanded every Jew to participate in its making because He wanted every Jewish person to have a part in the *Aron*, which symbolizes the Torah.

My Heart Is for You

Parshas Pekudei

וַיַּעַשׂ אֶת הַחֹשֶׁן (לט, ח–כא)
He made the *Choshen*.

R. Aryeh Levine was known for his concern for other people. He carried their burdens as if they were his own. We are all familiar with the time he went with his wife to the doctor because her foot was hurting. When they arrived at the doctor's office, R. Aryeh Levine said, "Doctor, my wife's foot hurts us!"

He also used to stand outside Yeshivas Eitz Chaim in Yerushalayim and examine the *cheder* boys as they entered the classroom.[126] Once his son asked him, "Tatty, why are you always watching the *cheder* boys so intently?" R. Aryeh Levine responded, "Take a look for yourself. What do you see?"

His son commented, "Wow, I can already tell who is eager to learn and who is not." To this, R. Aryeh Levine responded, "I see something different altogether. That child's pants are torn. This one's shoes are quite tattered and worn. That boy over there is definitely hungry." After which, he would do all that was in his power to aid them.[127]

R. Aryeh Levine dedicated his life to others. He was known as the

126 He was the *mashgiach* there.
127 *A Tzaddik in our Time*, pg. 319.

"Father of Prisoners" for his visits to members of the Jewish underground who were imprisoned during the British Mandate. He was also known as the "*Tzaddik* of Yerushalayim" for helping the poor and sick.

Aharon haKohen also personified this *middah*.[128] It was his selfless heart that enabled him to feel the pain and joy of others, as well as to worry about their issues.

When Moshe was chosen to be the leader of Klal Yisroel, the Torah testifies that Aharon's heart was filled with heartfelt joy for Moshe.[129] Even though Aharon was the older brother, there was no jealousy, resentment, or even animosity towards Moshe; only a heart filled with extreme happiness!

Chazal tell us that Aharon was *zocheh* to wear the *Choshen* — with the *Urim v'Tumim* inside of it — on his heart because of its purity.[130] The *Kohen* would ask the *Urim v'Tumim* a question on behalf of Klal Yisroel and the letters on the *Choshen* would illuminate in response. The *Kohen* would then decipher the message and explain what Hashem's reply was.[131] In order for the *Kohen* to be able to read the message correctly, he needed a heart that could feel and understand the pain of every Jew as well as see things objectively.[132] Aharon excelled in this capability and that is why he was *zocheh* to have the *Urim v'Tumim* placed on his pure heart.

The heart is the place from where all of our desires stem. If a person's heart is self-centered, then all of his desires are for himself. However, when a person goes beyond his personal feelings and feels the feelings of his spouse, family, and friends, he will discover that he will want what they want because his heart feels what they feel. This will propel him to care for them and support them in whichever aspect of life they need to be supported: physically, financially, or emotionally.

---

128 *Avos* 1:12. Chazal tell us that he loved peace and pursued it with all his might.

129 *Shemos* 4:14.

130 Rashi on *Shemos*, ibid. Look in *Sichos Mussar*, *Tetzavei* 5732, 23.

131 Look in the Rambam, *klei hamikdash* 10:10.

132 In *Shmuel* 1:1, Eli haKohen did not interpret the message of the *Urim v'Turim* correctly. He mistakenly thought Chana was a drunkard. He had consulted the *Urim v' Tumim* for guidance and the letters ש,כ,ר,ה lit up. He assumed that the letters spelled the *shikorah*, a drunken women, but in truth it was spelling *keshairah*, she is worthy.

SEFER VAYIKRA

DEVELOPING OURSELVES

PARSHAS VAYIKRA

כִּי כָל שְׂאֹר וְכָל דְּבַשׁ לֹא תַקְטִירוּ... וְכָל קָרְבַּן... בַּמֶּלַח תִּמְלָח (ב, יא–יג)
You should not bring ...any yeast or honey...you should salt...

So many people are occupied with trying to be somebody they're not. Once they fail to find themselves internally, they begin to search externally. Some people become professional imitators, others identify themselves with their acquisitions — be it a car, phone, home, or computer. However, *Yiddishkeit* is about being who we are, with the innate talents that we were given.

This reminds me of the famous story of when R. Naftali Amsterdam said to R. Yisroel Salanter, "If I only had the [very sharp and brilliant] mind of the *Shaagas Aryeh*, the heart of the *Yesod V'Shorash Ha'avoda*, and the character traits of Rebi, R. Yisroel Salanter, then I would be able to serve Hashem." R. Yisroel answered him, "Naftali, Naftali, only with your mind, your heart, and your character traits will you be able to serve Hashem, not with anybody else's."[133]

During the times of the Beis Hamikdash, we were not permitted to add yeast or honey to a *korban minchah*.[134] Both yeast and honey

133 Brought in *Alei Shor*, vol. 1, pg. 37.
134 A meal-offering.

are external additives. Yeast causes dough to rise higher, and honey makes it taste sweeter. Salt, though, an additive that brings out the natural flavor of the food, was permitted.

This, says R. Gifter, symbolizes what we just mentioned.[135]

When serving Hashem we should follow the model of salt and serve Him with our own innate attributes, and not with the ones that we have copied from others. We should liken ourselves to a dough that can stand on its own and does not need to borrow external additives in order to make it look and taste good.

Hashem never asked us to be something that we are not, however, He does expect us to be who we are. We do this by bringing our intrinsic potential to fruition in the service of Hashem, and that is what *Yiddishkeit* is about: you becoming you.

We dip our bread into salt at meals to remind us of the *korbanos* that were brought on the *Mizbe'ach*. Perhaps this act can also remind us about ourselves. Just as salt brings out the natural flavors of a food, so too we should bring our G-d-given talents and character traits to fruition.[136]

---

135 Reprinted with special permission from R. Zelig Pliskin, *Growth through Torah*, in the name of R. Gifter, *Pirkei Torah*, vol. 1, pg. 1.

136 See below on *Parshas Shemini*.

OUR DEEP-SEATED LOYALTY TO HASHEM

PARSHAS VAYIKRA

וְהִקְרִיב מִן הַתֹּרִים אוֹ מִן בְּנֵי הַיּוֹנָה (א, יד)

He shall bring his offering from the *turim* doves or from the *benei yonah* doves.

The following is an excerpt from the testimony of Rivkah Cooper, an Auschwitz survivor, at the Eichmann trial in Yerushalayim:[137]

Birkenau, 1943. When we arrived in Birkenau on January 18, 1943, one of the first things we did was search for something we might use as Shabbos *licht*. We were successful in improvising two candles and with a group of ten or twelve girls, we stealthily kindled the *licht* on *erev* Shabbos. When we began to sing softly the Shabbos *zemiros*, women gathered from all corners of our cellblock to join us. Some of them were weeping, while others begged us for permission to make a *brachah* on our *licht*.

Every *erev* Shabbos thereafter, this became a ritual in

137 *Justice in Jerusalem* (New York: Harper and Row, 1966), pg. 190.

> our cellblock. Often, we had no food, at times no water to drink, but somehow we managed to obtain what was needed to kindle our Shabbos *licht*. The same held true for every *chag*. True, we had no matzos for Pesach, but somehow we managed to obtain potatoes, and thereby avoided eating any *chametz*. We even fasted on Yom Kippur in Auschwitz.

The Ramban links the Jew's innate loyalty and devotion to the bird offerings mentioned in this week's *parshah*.

There are only two types of birds that can be used as a *korban olah*:[138] a *turim* dove and a *benei yonah* dove. The *turim* doves are only acceptable once they have fully matured, and the *benei yonah* doves are only acceptable while they are young.[139] What message lies within these perplexing laws?

The Ramban says that these two types of doves share a common attribute of loyalty.[140] The *turim* dove's loyalty is only evident once it has matured and found a mate, whereas the *benei yonah* dove's loyalty is only evident while it is still a baby.

Turim doves are everlastingly loyal to their mates. Even after its mate dies, the *turim* doves will mourn its loss forever, never seeking another mate. The Ramban explains that just as the *turim* dove clings to its mate and will never leave it for another, so too the Jewish soul clings to Hashem and will never leave Him for another deity. That is why Hashem only wants the mature *turim* doves for a *korban* because they represent this loyalty. Perhaps we can add that this representation aids in arousing Hashem's attribute of love and compassion, which in turn brings atonement.

The Ramban notes further that *benei yonah* doves also share this attribute of loyalty; however, their loyalty is not to a mate but to their nest. Chazal tell us that if a person tries to take eggs or baby chicks from a nest, most birds will immediately abandon their nest. The only exception to this rule is the *benei yonah* dove, in whom Hashem

---

138 An elevation offering, which is completely consumed on the *Mizbe'ach*.

139 *Rashi* on *Vayikra* 1:14.

140 Ramban, ibid.

instilled a deep feeling of attachment to its nest. This feeling causes them to never abandon it — even if a person tampers with it.[141]

The *benei yonah* dove symbolizes our attachment to Hashem and His Torah. Just as *benei yonah* doves are born with this feeling of attachment towards their nests, so too every Jew is born with an instinctive feeling of attachment to Hashem and His Torah. This feeling of attachment does not allow the Jew to forsake Hashem, no matter what is at stake. Even if the Jew is coerced to convert or forsake Hashem and His Torah, he will be there to fight with all his might and never let go.

Deep inside every Jew sits a deep loyalty to Hashem and His Torah. True, some have it hidden from them and others feel it rise to the surface when their *Yiddishkeit* is being threatened. Fortunate is one who is able to live with it every single day.

---

141 Even though the *benei yonah* doves remain attached to their nests, even when they have matured, nonetheless when they mature they develop a negative attribute of jealousy towards other birds, which causes them to be disloyal to their mates.

Appreciating What We Have

Parshas Vayikra

וְאִם לֹא תַגִּיעַ יָדוֹ...שְׁתֵּי תֹרִים אוֹ שְׁנֵי בְנֵי יוֹנָה לַה' אֶחָד לְחַטָּאת וְאֶחָד לְעֹלָה (ה, ז)

But if his means are insufficient... he shall bring two *turim* doves or two *benei yonah*, one for a sin-offering and one for an *olah*-offering.

This week's *parshah* addresses the *korban olah ve'yored* — the "ascending and descending offering" — a *korban* that goes "up and down." It does not mean that the *Kohanim* shake the *korban* up and down; rather it is called this because its costs vary according to what the sinner can afford. A rich man must bring an animal as his *korban* and a poor man could bring a bird. The halachah dictates that every time a poor person brings his *korban olah ve'yored*, he has to bring an additional bird along with it as a *korban olah*.[142]

This additional *korban* needs an explanation. Why does the poor person have to bring a *korban olah* in addition to his *korban olah ve'yored,* while the rich person fulfills his obligation with only one *korban*? If the Torah is concerned about the poor man's financial

142 An elevation offering.

status, why does it require him to bring a second bird?

R. Simcha Ziskind Brody,[143] the late Rosh Yeshiva of Yeshivas Chevron, elaborates on an Ibn Ezra that gives us the key to this mystery.[144]

People who bring *korbanos* to Hashem want to bring honorable and respectable ones, especially if they are seeking atonement. When a poor person realizes that he cannot afford an honorable and respectable animal and has to downgrade himself to a "meager" bird, he may have feelings of animosity in his heart towards Hashem. He may even be thinking, "Why didn't Hashem let me bring a rich man's *korban*? Why did I have to bring a meager bird?" Such thoughts are considered an *aveirah* and need atonement. On the chance that the poor person had such thoughts, the Torah obligates him to bring as well a *korban olah*, which atones for wrong thoughts.

Although the opportunity for a poor person to bring a bird as a *korban* is a *chessed* from Hashem, nonetheless we see that some poor people find it hard to come to terms with such a *chessed*. Maybe it was the "grass is always greener on the other side" plague that blinded them from their own blessings or perhaps they were embittered due to their poverty.

Whatever the reason might be, we all must remember that along with poverty and wealth, our entire existence is in the hands of Hashem. He gives every single person precisely what he needs, when he needs it, and how he needs it, for his own best. To measure oneself with somebody else's measuring stick only brings disappointment and does not allow one to appreciate what he has. If only this poor person would realize that Hashem understood his plight, sympathized with him, and even invented a new halachah to accommodate his situation, he would feel indebted to Hashem for the love and concern shown to him.

R. Avigdor Miller was known for finding appreciation and happiness with the "minor things" that most people take for granted, like eating, sleeping, walking, and talking. One time R. Miller's grandson

143 *Saam Derech, Vayikra*, pg. 240.
144 5:7.

found R. Miller with his head in a sink filled with water. He called out in alarm, "*Zeide, Zeide*, is everything all right?" R. Miller picked up his head from the water and answered him with a smile, "My dear grandchild, everything is wonderful. I had just forgotten how wonderful it was to breathe, so I put my head in a sink filled with water to remind myself."

Life itself and everything that comes along with it is a precious gift from Hashem. No matter what one's situation might be, one has to know and believe that Hashem has our best interests in mind and is bestowing upon us endless goodness every single second of the day. Let the poor man's additional *korban olah* remind us that we have exactly what we are supposed to have, and in that way we will discover how "rich" we really are.[145]

145 Parenthetically, we can see how much one's thoughts play a role in the Torah's establishment of law, meaning to say that the Torah understands the psyche of the poor man and because of it creates a new halachah: the obligation for a poor person to bring a *korban olah* as well. Fascinating!

OTHER PEOPLE'S DIGNITY

PARSHAS TZAV

בִּמְקוֹם אֲשֶׁר תִּשָּׁחֵט הָעֹלָה תִּשָּׁחֵט הַחַטָּאת (ו,יח)

In the place where the *korban olah* is slaughtered,[146] the *korban chatas* (sin offering) shall be slaughtered.

Rashi enlightens us as to why the Torah wants the *korban chatas*, a sin offering, to be slaughtered in the very same place as the *korban olah*, a voluntary offering.[147]

He explains that Hashem is concerned about a sinner's dignity and honor.[148] Just imagine how the offender would feel if there was a designated place in the Beis Hamikdash solely for people who had to bring a *korban chatas*, a *korban* that atoned for severe transgression. Most probably all the sinners would turn white as ghosts from shame and humiliation. In order to save them from that humiliation, Hashem said that the *korban chatas* should be slaughtered in the very same place as the *korban olah*. That way, nobody would be able

146 A *korban olah* can be a voluntary *korban*, which is completely consumed on the *Mizbe'ach*.

147 There are times when a person is obligated to bring a *korban olah* — for example after a wrong thought — however it can also be brought voluntarily.

148 This Rashi is found in Rashi's *siddur* number 21. It is also brought in the *Moisif Rashi*, found in the *Mikraos Gedolos haMaor*.

to detect if the *korban* was brought on account of a transgression or if it was brought voluntarily, since a *korban olah* can be brought voluntarily.

The more one contemplates and internalizes the idea that Rashi is teaching us, the more considerate and caring one could become. The sinner that the Torah is referring to did not respect Hashem or His Torah, and yet Hashem respected him and saved him from humiliation by hiding his wrongdoing from others.

Here we have a vivid example of how cautious one must be regarding his friend's pride and honor. Even if somebody insulted or offended another, the insulted one is not permitted to insult, offend, or embarrass the one who insulted him. On the contrary, he must try and save him from any future embarrassment.

R. Shneur Kotler once led a group of *rabbonim* to Eretz Yisroel in order to take care of a pressing issue for Klal Yisroel. When they arrived, they ran into some opposition that publicly ridiculed and insulted R. Shneur. As per his personality, R. Shneur did not take any offense and continued his pursuit to aid the *Kehal*.

When R. Shneur was in New York, he saw the person who had publicly embarrassed him months prior. R. Shneur immediately ran over to him, gave him a big *shalom a'leichem*, and invited him to Lakewood for Shabbos. The man declined the offer, but R. Shneur persisted until he finally agreed. R. Shneur gave him the honor of speaking in the yeshiva on Shabbos and treated him with the utmost respect. In R. Shneur's eyes, he was doing nothing more than what a regular *ben Torah* is supposed to do, while in our eyes he was acting like a *Gadol*.

R. Shneur was walking in the ways of Hashem. Just as Hashem is concerned for the dignity and honor of the people who disrespect Him, R. Shneur was concerned for the man who embarrassed him.[149]

What a lesson for all of us!

---

149 Look in *Otzeros haTorah* on *Parshas Kedoshim*, where you will find a similar story about R. Yisroel Salanter with a different lesson.

PEANUT BUTTER ON THE WALLS

PARSHAS TZAV

בִּמְקוֹם אֲשֶׁר תִּשָּׁחֵט הָעֹלָה תִּשָּׁחֵט הַחַטָּאת (ו, יח)
In the place where the *korban olah* is slaughtered, the *korban chatas* shall be slaughtered.

Mr. Ben-Oliel was beside himself when he came home and found a brand new, one pound jar of Skippy peanut butter smeared all over the wall of one of the childrens' bedrooms. He decided that he had to get to the bottom of things. Although he was rather upset, he still managed to contain himself and succeeded in confronting each child in a diplomatic manner.

Over the course of the day, Mr. Ben-Oliel invited each of his children separately into the "vandalized" bedroom to play a game (he covered the wall in a way that the peanut butter was not visible). All of them entered the bedroom separately with a smile and enjoyed a few quiet minutes with Tatty. That is, all except for little six-year-old Moshe, who was avoiding Tatty. He refused to go into the bedroom and none of his siblings understood his hesitation. Finally, Mr. Ben-Oliel went to get Moshe himself. They both sat down together and started to talk.

It took about five minutes for Moshe to confess and understand that what he did was wrong, and about ten minutes for Mr. Ben-Oliel and Moshe to clean up the wall together. What could have been a catastrophe turned into a great day of "father-son" bonding.

The Torah says that the *korban chatas* (a sin offering) is to be slaughtered in the very same place as the *korban olah* (a voluntary offering).

Chazal learn from here a timeless lesson when it comes to being sensitive to other people's feelings. They explain that the reason why Hashem designated the same place for these *korbanos* was to prevent embarrassment and shame to a sinner who was coming with his *korban chatas* – sin offering – to repent. If everybody knew what kind of *korban* he was bringing, he would feel very embarrassed and ashamed when bringing it to the Beis Hamikdash.[150]

In order to prevent this from happening, Hashem said that the *korban chatas* should be slaughtered in the very same place as the *korban olah*. This way, nobody would know that the sinner was bringing a *korban chatas* to atone for his misdeeds. Perhaps he was a person who benevolently volunteered a *korban olah*.[151] Hence, the *pasuk* is teaching us not to even embarrass sinners who have come to repent, just as Hashem has saved sinners from embarrassment.

In our aforementioned story, not only did Mr. Ben-Oliel find the culprit, but he did it in a diplomatic way that did not embarrass his little Moshe.

When parents see their children doing something wrong, it is very easy for them to react inappropriately and cause embarrassment to the guilty child in front of his or her siblings. Not only does this make it difficult for the child to admit to his wrongdoing and accept the rebuke, but even more so, it could embarrass him.

It is important to get to the bottom of things, but it is even more important to consider other people's feeling and do it in a dignified manner that will not cause the wrongdoer any emotional harm.

---

150 *Yerushalmi, Yevamos* 8:3. It is also brought in *Bavli, Sotah* 32b.

151 This Rashi is found is Rashi's *siddur* ch. 21. It is also brought in the *Moisif Rashi,* which is found in the *Mikraos Gedolos haMaor*.

LEARN HOW TO TAKE THE BLAME

PARSHAS SHEMINI

וַיְהִי בַּיּוֹם הַשְּׁמִינִי (ט, א)
It was on the eighth day.

It was *Rosh Chodesh* Nissan. The inauguration of the *Mishkan* had just been completed and the *Shechinah* had not yet descended. Aharon haKohen was very disheartened as he told Moshe, "I am to blame. Hashem is still angry with me because of the *Chet haEgel* and that is why the *Shechinah* has not come." Only after Moshe and Aharon went into the *Ohel Mo'ed* and asked Hashem for mercy did the *Shechinah* descend.[152]

We see something extraordinary in Aharon haKohen, says R. Yeruchem Levovits.[153] When problems arise, many people tend to blame the circumstances or other people, but certainly not themselves. Especially when the problems affect a lot of people, it is easy to blame everything else except oneself. Aharon haKohen did just the opposite; he placed the entire blame on himself! This is something extraordinary that needs an explanation.

152 Look in *Rashi* on 9:23.
153 *Daas Torah*.

This question can be extended to the Purim story as well. The Vilna Gaon explains that the reason Mordechai cried a loud and bitter cry was because Mordechai felt that he was the sole cause for Klal Yisroel's pending annihilation![154] This is also perplexing. How was Mordechai, "the savior of Klal Yisroel," the only one to blame for the evil decree? Surely Klal Yisroel's participation in the *seudah* had something to do with it.[155]

Maybe we can understand this with the help of the Ramban.[156] The Ramban teaches us that when a person wants to measure himself, the measuring stick is not how he compares to his friends and peers, but rather how he compares to himself.[157] How much have I developed, grown, and changed, rather than how much better am I than them? The reason for this is because one who measures himself against his peers will always find people "smaller" than him, and hence his assessment of himself will be inaccurate. In addition, he will lack the motivation to better himself because he will always find somebody else to blame.

Even though Aharon haKohen and Mordechai were on such high levels, they still held themselves accountable for what was happening only because they measured themselves against themselves. Aharon was not pretending to take "the blame"; rather he discovered something within himself that might have caused the tragedy.[158] If he would have measured himself against his peers instead of discovering his faults,[159] he might have found the faults of others, blamed them, felt that his slate was clean and would have lost an opportunity to become that much better.

In truth, although measuring oneself against one's peers seeming-

154 See his commentary on *Esther* 4:1.

155 The meal that Achashveirosh made.

156 Based on my understanding of the *Igeres haRamban*. Look in the *Chovos Halevavos, Sha'ar Hakenia*, ch. 10.

157 Look in the *Chovos Halevavos, Sha'ar Yichud Hamaiysa*, ch. 5, s.v. *"Al ken, al tatridcha meilchamas zulaso* etc."

158 Perhaps Aharon felt that he was to blame because he continuously lived with "his *chet*," the *Chet haEgal*.

159 Aharon and Mordechai were on levels so high that we cannot begin to fathom. We are writing just to learn from them how to become better people.

ly cleans one's slate, it also has its setbacks.[160] More often than not, when looking at others, we discover their talents and accomplishments that we do not have. This blinds us from discovering our own talents and accomplishments. As a result, we feel inadequate and view ourselves as underachievers.

Every one of us is unique. Hashem graced all of us with individualized talents and abilities that make us all different. If we would only realize that we are all unique with our own personalities, lifestyles, and families, we might begin to understand that measuring oneself against oneself is not only a good idea — it is imperative.

We all need a personal measuring stick. We learn from Aharon that true growth comes from measuring oneself against oneself. This will enable us to discover areas within ourselves that we can still work on and perfect. On top of that, we will discover our own personal uniqueness in serving Hashem and find that internal happiness that we are all searching for.

160 Based on *Alei Shor*, vol. 1, pg. 34.

OVERCOMING SELF-IMPOSED LIMITATIONS

PARSHAS SHEMINI

קְרַב אֶל הַמִּזְבֵּחַ (ט, ז)
Come near to the *Mizbe'ach*.

Seven days of dismantling and reassembling the *Mishkan* had transpired and the *Shechinah* still had not yet come. It was seven days of effort without results. Aharon haKohen took the blame and said to Moshe, "Hashem is still upset with me and the *Shechinah* has not come because of my mistake!"[161]

The Ramban writes that Aharon haKohen only had one sin — the *Chet haEgel* — and it was so minuscule that we cannot even fathom what it was. Nonetheless, he lived with it constantly.

Now it was the eighth day of the inauguration of the *Mishkan* and it was Aharon's turn to offer up the *korbanos*. Moshe turned to him and told him to proceed as planned. Aharon hesitated. Moshe questioned him, "Why are you so embarrassed? What is your hesitation? This is what you were created for!" Moshe rightfully believed that the *Shechinah* was waiting for Aharon to offer up his *korbanos*.

161 Look in *Rashi* on 9:23 and in the Ramban there.

However, it was easier said than done. Aharon had a mighty hurdle to climb. Aside for his internal turmoil, there was something else he had to overcome. Hashem gave permission to the *yetzer hara* to make the *Mizbe'ach* appear like a golden calf![162]

Nonetheless, despite what Aharon believed in his mind and what was staring him straight in the face, a living golden calf, he accepted the command of Moshe and proceeded further. Chazal tell us he proceeded with zest and as soon as he finished, the *Shechinah* came. This showed Klal Yisroel that Aharon was truly loved by Hashem and was chosen by Hashem to be the *Kohen Gadol.*

It amazes me to think about how much inner strength he had to muster up in order to overcome himself, his shame, and his humility — not to mention the image that appeared in front of him.

How many of our limitations are self-imposed? How many of us think that we cannot when in truth we can? The lesson here is clear. Even the great Aharon haKohen, on his level, had what we call limitations. The difference is that he managed to overcome them. Now it is our turn.[163]

162 Look at the Ramban here.

163 Based on the *Saam Derech.*

BIRD CARE

PARSHAS TAZRIA

וּבֶן יוֹנָה אוֹ תֹר (יב, ו)
And a *benei yonah* dove or a *turim* dove.

After about forty-five minutes of searching for some firewood, Yaakov and Eli finally found the perfect log. Yaakov went to call his older brother to help them lift it while Eli stayed to watch the log. By the time Yaakov returned with his older brother, Eli had wandered off and had forgotten where it was. Yaakov just smiled at Eli and said, "Oh, it doesn't matter Eli, I am sure we will find another one."

By choosing to make the lost log inconsequential and by overlooking Eli's mistake, Yaakov succeeded in saving Eli from feelings of failure and shame.

If our priority is other people's feelings, then it is easy to do this.

After a new mother gives birth, she is obligated to bring a *korban chatas* to the Beis Hamikdash.[164] She can either bring a *ben yonah* dove or a *tur* dove as her *korban*. The Baal haTurim notices an inconsistency in the order of how the Torah lists these birds. Usually

164 She is obligated to bring two *korbanos* to the Beis Hamikdash, a *korban oleh ve'yored* and a *korban chatas*.

the *tur* dove is mentioned first and the *ben yonah* dove afterward. However, here by the new mother, they are reversed. Why is that?

The answer is that the new mother's *korban* is the only *korban* that consists of one dove, whereas every other person who is obligated to bring such a *korban* must bring two doves. The Torah switched the order to tell us that the preferred bird to use in this situation is the *benei yonah* dove.

The reason is that the *tur* doves are totally devoted to their mates,[165] and if the new mother would bring a *tur* dove as her *korban*, its remaining mate would mourn its loss forever. That is why the Torah changes the order of the birds listed only by the new mother's *korban*: to teach us that it is better for her to bring a *benei yonah* dove in order to prevent pain to the *tur* dove.

The Torah is teaching us the importance of other people's feelings and what level of concern and sensitivity is demanded from us. If we are concerned with the well-being of birds, as well as respecting their faithfulness to one another, all the more should we be concerned for other people's feelings.[166]

Especially during these holy days of *Sefiras haOmer*, when 24,000 students of Rabbi Akiva passed away because they did not show the proper respect to one another, we should try to honor our friends and family as best as we can; in particular our wives, since the Rambam writes that we should honor them more than we honor ourselves.

We just caught a glimpse of the sensitivities that the Torah portrays. It is truly the path of goodness. Hashem gave us such a wonderful gift. Let us cherish it!

---

165 Parenthetically speaking, the Ramban teaches us that the *ben yonah* dove also has an attribute of loyalty, not to her mate but rather to her nest, never leaving it. It is for that reason, explains the Ramban, why the bird offering is either a *tur* dove or a *ben yonah* dove, because they both show signs of loyalty, just like the Jewish people are always loyal to the Torah and Hashem. See above on *Parshas Vayikra*, "Our Deep-Seated Loyalty to Hashem."

166 R. Simcha Ziskin Brody in *Saam Derech*.

JUST ONE WORD

PARSHAS TAZRIA

וְרָאָהוּ הַכֹּהֵן וְטִמֵּא אֹתוֹ (יג, ד)

The Kohen should look at it and make him *tamei*.

Many people speak *lashon hara* out of ignorance, as they often think, "What did I do after all? I only said a few words."

Who would have thought that one little word could pack such a punch? Well, the *parshah* of *tzaraas* teaches us otherwise.

As soon as the *kohen* declares one word — *tamei* — the *metzora* is sent into isolation, and when he then declares that other one word — *tahor* — the *metzora* is taken out. This is there to teach us the potential that lies behind even one word.

In addition to how the *metzora* becomes *tamei* is him actually being *tamei*. The *metzora* suffers in total isolation with painful and embarrassing *tzaraas* all over his body until he rectifies his ways. All this pain and suffering is on account of those few words of *lashon hara* that he spoke. The Dubner Maggid writes that the *metzora* should not think that he was dealt with unfairly, because his punishment fits the crime.[167]

---

167 *Ohel Yaakov*, the beginning of *Parshas Metzorah*, s.v. "*Zos*."

The Dubner Maggid also writes that even if a person succeeded in speaking *lashon hara* without harming the person he was speaking about, he nonetheless harms himself. The prosecuting attorneys in Heaven can only prosecute us once we have spoken *lashon hara*. The more we speak, the more they are permitted to prosecute. If we never spoke a word of *lashon hara*, they would never be permitted to open their mouths. Again, we see that one word can make a difference.

Today, people take all kinds of tiny pills for their health. Ask a man who is taking a pill for his heart condition to skip for a couple of days. If he is not willing to stop, try to reason with him by saying that it is only one little pill. Chances are you will not get too far. We see that even small things are sometimes very big.

On the flip side, one word can also be used to encourage, inspire, comfort, and heal, as Shlomo haMelech said: "Life and death are in the tongue's hands."[168]

A parent's "I'm so proud of you" or "You did great" can boost a child for weeks. A struggling student who gets back a test marked "Excellent" now has the encouragement to keep striving. If we hurt somebody, we can heal the pain by asking for forgiveness. We can create new relationships and enhance our preexisting ones with just a pleasant hello.

We all have experienced it and can testify to the fact that one positive word really can make a difference.

The power of speech is one of the millions of precious assets that Hashem has given to humanity.[169] It is what separates and raises us above the animals. Let's try to remember to use it and not abuse it.

---

168 *Mishlei* 18:21.

169 Look in *Chovos Halevavos, Sha'ar Habechinah*, ch. 5, *"Ve'acharkach cheshev be'mah she'hetiv bo...be'dibor."*

RIDING THROUGH THE STORM

PARSHAS METZORA

וְעָשָׂה הַכֹּהֵן אֶת הַחַטָּאת וְכִפֶּר (יד, יט)

The *kohen* shall perform the *chatas* service and provide atonement.

Aside for the anxiety of having such a frightening disease overtake his life, the *metzora* had to endure feelings of shame, humiliation, and loneliness during his days of solitary confinement.[170]

However, despite the *metzora's* plight, he too is obligated to face every situation with *emunah*, to understand and believe that even in the darkest and most painful circumstances that everything is from Hashem and that nothing bad can possibly come from Him. On the contrary, only goodness emanates from Him.

Unfortunately, this was not the case with every *metzora*. The Ramban understands that in addition to the atonement needed for speaking *lashon hara*, the *metzora* was also required to bring an additional *korban* to atone for the thoughts that he might have had while being a *metzora*.[171]

---

170 This complete isolation, being away from his friends and family, was part of his healing process.

171 The word כפר, which means atonement, is mentioned three times by the *met-*

The Ramban suggests that the pained *metzora* might have accidentally "blamed" Hashem for "wronging" him. "Was the *lashon hara* really that bad?" "Why do I have to suffer so much?" "Why does Hashem have to be so mean and put me through such torture?" For such thoughts to pass through a Jew's mind, even somebody whose life is filled with pain and anguish like the *metzora*, is a grave and awful sin.

Practically speaking, not being able to see the whole picture can cause a person to, *chas v'shalom*, think judgmentally towards Hashem. Many of us have our daily doses of inconveniences and problems. Our duty as a Jew is not to question Hashem or His actions, but rather to seek out the good in everything He sends us, accept our difficulties lovingly and believe that all of our situations are handcrafted for our best. This is true even if one is found in the grimmest and most painful of situations, similar to that of the *metzora*.[172]

It is reassuring to know that such *emunah* lives and exists within all of us. R. Chaim of Volozhin teaches us that we are blessed with the ability to accept lovingly anything that befalls us.[173] This ability was bequeathed to us as a spiritual inheritance from Avraham Avinu.

As Avraham Avinu passed his trials and tribulations, he imbued *emunah* into the Jewish DNA. He was promised fame and wealth and walked into a famine. He was told that Yitzchok would be his only predecessor and then was told to slaughter him. Avraham never asked questions or judged Hashem, but rather lived with perfect faith in Hashem and His infinite goodness. His *emunah* was embedded into every Jew soul. Our job is to find that *emunah* and bring it to fruition.[174]

There once was a *rebbe* crying for the *geulah* because the *Yidden* were suffering too much. A *chassid* standing by asked his *rebbe*, "But Rebbe, we believe that Hashem will not give us more than we can handle!" To that the *rebbe* replied, "That's precisely why I

---

zora's korbanos. This implies that the *metzora* did three things wrong.

172 Based on *Saam Derech*, pg. 75.

173 Look in *Ruach Chaim* 5:2, and above on *Parshas Lech Lecha*.

174 Look at *Sifsei Chaim*, *Moadim*, vol. 2, pg. 419.

am crying. Because of our strong *emunah*, we could handle almost anything."

Life is filled with its challenges and surprises; let us learn from the laws of the *metzora* and Avraham Avinu how a Jew is supposed to walk through those trying times with his or her *emunah* escorting him or her every step of the way.

PLANNING FOR THE FUTURE

PARSHAS ACHAREI MOS

וּשְׁמַרְתֶּם אֶת חֻקֹּתַי... וָחַי בָּהֶם (יח, ה)

You shall observe My decrees...by which he shall live.

The little village of Zallva, a suburb of Grodna, Russia, was famous for its yearly trade fair. For four weeks out of the year, thousands of merchants and consumers would come from far and wide in order to partake in the fair's fabulous deals. Some merchants would even rent tiny and decrepit rooms for the duration of the fair just to be able to participate.

During those four weeks, the merchants would work around the clock selling their wares, as most of them would earn their yearly income from those four weeks.

Although much fatigue and many unpleasantries accompanied their extra workload, they still managed to work until they could not work anymore, because more work meant more money, and more money meant more rest and relaxation in the upcoming year.

One year, the great Chafetz Chaim was visiting Zallva during the fair and witnessed an exchange between a stand owner and his employee.

"*Oy,*" mumbled the employee. "I am so exhausted and just want to sleep in a normal bed! When is the dreadful fair going to end?"

"Fool!" the stand owner remarked. "*Halevai* the fair would last another four weeks. It is true that we are all tired and weary, but think about how much money we are making every day. We are working for the whole year, and when the fair is over, we will all be millionaires!"

The stand owner's words rang in the Chafetz Chaim's ears.

"Did you hear what you just said?" interrupted the Chafetz Chaim. "It is worthwhile for a person to work night and day and live in subhuman conditions with sheer exhaustion for a short period of time in order to reap the fruit of his labor afterward. Moreover," added the Chafetz Chaim, "I see that the more a person is entirely focused on his glorious future, the less he will feel his present pain and exhaustion. On the contrary, he will accept them lovingly, knowing that his pain and efforts are the way to his tremendous eternal pleasure."

To this, the Chafetz Chaim concluded how fortunate is the one who understands that this world, *Olam Hazeh*, is also like a trade fair. It is a temporary dwelling place where we can amass an enormous amount of spiritual money, our Torah and mitzvos, for our real eternal home in *Olam Haba*. With such an outlook, a person will be able to tolerate the pain and discomfort that comes from the unpleasantries of this world and will even be willing to work around the clock for his eternal home in *Olam Haba*, just as the merchants did in the fair.

CARRYING YOUR OWN BAG OF DIAMONDS

PARSHAS ACHAREI MOS

וָחַי בָּהֶם — ולא שימות בהם (יח, ה)
By which he shall live.

Eli Bringman was a *shlepper*, a moving man, who was hired to carry somebody's bag of priceless diamonds. As he slipped the diamonds into his pocket, he was filled with excitement. "Wow, priceless diamonds," he thought, "this is so exciting." However, after some time the bag started to get a bit uncomfortable in his pocket and he began to sweat. Carrying those diamonds was not as glorious as he thought.[175]

How do you think Eli would have felt if they were his diamonds? Do you thing that the sweat would have bothered him at all? I think we can all agree that he would have been more than ecstatic to carry his own diamonds. However, the reality is that he was a *shlepper* and that they were not his diamonds, but rather belonged to the person who hired him to carry them.

When it comes to our *avodas Hashem*, we must decide if we are

175 Look in *B'zoes Ani Boteach* from Maran HaRav Shach *zt"l*, pg. 34–40.

carrying our own bag of diamonds or if we are being hired out by Hashem to carry His bag of diamonds. If we are carrying Hashem's bag, then chances are they will become heavy after sometime. However, if they are our own, we will enjoy them every minute of the day.

There are *Yidden* who truly want to serve Hashem, just they have a very big *yetzer hara* that tries to pull them in every other direction except for the right one. There are also *Yidden* who feel as if they are doing Hashem a favor by carrying His bags. They truly wish that they could do whatever their heart desires, just they cannot because they have to serve Hashem.

On the surface, both groups basically look the same. They both wake up for *davening* and make *brachos*. However, if we would free them of their shackles and chains, they would end up in very different universes. One would actualize his dream by becoming the best *eved Hashem* he could be, while the other would live a life of sheer self-indulgence.

Along with everything in the world, people who do things because they want to will find joy in what they do, while the people who do things because they have to are nothing more than *shleppers* carrying somebody else's bag of diamonds. It might be exciting at the beginning, but in the end could be nothing more than an uncomfortable bag that belongs to somebody else, causing them to sweat.[176]

---

176 Based on *Chochma U'mussar*, 2:127.

UNCONDITIONAL LOVE

PARSHAS ACHAREI MOS

הַשֹּׁכֵן אִתָּם בְּתוֹךְ טֻמְאֹתָם (טז, טז)
The One that dwells with them amidst their *tumah*.

In July 2014, Hamas, an Arab terrorist organization, shot over two thousand missiles within a period of two weeks into Eretz Yisroel. Miraculously only one Jew was killed.[177]

If we could imagine all of the Hamas leaders sitting around a table smoking their pipes as they were planning their attack, perhaps it would look something like this:

"Okay. If we shoot two thousand missiles into Israel, even in the worst case scenario, each missile only kills one Jew, that is two thousand Jews dead. Ha ha ha, wonderful. Let's do it." The joke, however, is on them. Hashem foiled their plans as He came to our rescue once again.

Hashem's love for us is unconditional. Despite our gigantic *pekel* of imperfections and impurities, Hashem still loves us and is taking care of us. Miraculous!

177 I don't like to use the word "only," because every Jew is precious and worth millions, and in truth it is one Jew too many. I just mean to stress the power of the miracle.

The verse above,[178] "The One that dwells with them amidst their *tumah*," teaches us that even if a person accidentally enters into the Beis Hamikdash in his contaminated, impure state, Hashem will not leave. Even such disrespect and offensiveness cannot chase Him away because He loves us too much to leave.[179]

After catching glimpses of Hashem's unconditional love, we should be asking ourselves in what way can we show our love and appreciation or reciprocate this kindness back to Hashem? Let us not forget that we have a relationship with Him, and just like all relationships are a two-way street of giving and loving, so is this one. As soon as we recognize the goodness that He has sent us, it is our turn to reciprocate back with love and a thank you.

We can begin by saying a sincere thank you, but in truth the *Chovos Halevavos* writes that a Jew not only thanks with words, but also with action. When we live a Torah lifestyle and thereby fulfill Hashem's will, we are in essence saying thank you to Hashem with our actions, and hence building our relationship with Him that much more.[180]

---

178 *Vayikra* 16:16.

179 *Me'am Loez*.

180 One might ask: "Me, give love or reciprocation back to Hashem? Hashem does not need anything!" Perhaps we can liken it to a boy that had the richest father in the world. What could the boy possibly give to his father on his father's birthday? The boy came home from *cheder* with a bar of chocolate in his bag. He went up to his father and told him the following. "Tatty, this is my favorite chocolate in the whole world, and I got it because I memorized seventy-five *mishnayos b'al-peh*. I want you to have it for your birthday because I love you so much." Believe me, that chocolate bar is worth more than all the money in the world to his father. So too, when it comes to us giving to Hashem, we can *kaveyachol* give Him our love.

STAND UP TO YOUR OWN REBUKE

PARSHAS KEDOSHIM

הוֹכֵחַ תּוֹכִיחַ אֶת עֲמִיתֶךָ (יט, יז)
You shall rebuke your fellow.

The king sentenced Alex to death for theft — a rather large sentence for such a crime. Before the sentence was carried out, Alex requested permission to speak to the king and permission was granted.

He told the king that he had a vital piece of information that could better the world and to kill him without revealing it would be an injustice. Alex requested to teach the king what he knew before he was put to death.

The king was eager to hear more and told Alex to continue. He told the king that he knew how to make an enormous fruit tree, already bearing luscious fruits, sprout forth from the ground within half-an-hour after planting a seed. The king was so enthusiastic that he immediately invited his highest ranking officer and his treasurer to escort him and Alex to the garden to witness this astonishing feat.

Alex requested an apple, a bucket of water, and ten specific spices and minerals, all with their exact measure. Alex mixed everything together, cut open the apple, took out a seed and placed it into the mixture. After about twenty minutes, he announced, "The seed is ready to be planted. You are all about to witness the impossible. With my mixture I will be able to make an enormous fruit tree sprout out of the ground, already laden with its luscious fruits!"

"There is only one condition that I need your help with," Alex said to the king. "The tree will only grow if a person who is totally clean from theft plants the seed. I obviously cannot be the one, since I have stolen." He then turned to the king's highest-ranking officer and said, "Please sir, could you help me with the planting?"

The officer was taken off-guard and admitted that he too had stolen once and was also reluctant to be the one to plant the seed. Perhaps the miraculous feat would not work on account of him.

Alex then turned to the king's treasurer. "Please, honored and esteemed treasurer, help us by planting the seed." "Me?" replied the treasurer. "But I am appointed over all the king's wealth and fortune. Perhaps I too have made mistakes in my reckoning and do not have hands that are clean from theft either."

"O great King, you are the only one here who can be honored with the planting," said Alex as he handed the seed over to the king. The king too confessed and said that when he was younger he desired one of his father's diamonds and had stolen it. "Bring in somebody else," commanded the king.

In the midst of all the commotion, Alex threw himself to the mercy of the king and pleaded, "My master, my king; your best officer, your personal treasurer and even the king himself have admitted that their hands are not clean from theft. If so, why has the king placed upon me such a harsh sentence? I stole because I was starving in my poverty! Please pardon me and let me live!"

The king understood what Alex was trying to do, sympathized with him, and changed the verdict to a much lighter one.[181]

Chazal teach us that every time the word "*es*" appears in the Torah

---

181 The essay was taken from *Otzeros Hatorah*, courtesy of the author, Harav Eliyahu Chaim Cohen *shlita*, in the name of the Ben Eish Chai.

it comes to include something that was not stated explicitly in the *pasuk*. R. Yisroel Salanter writes that the *es* of our *pasuk*, "*Hoche'ach toche'ach es amisecha*," comes to include oneself. We learn from here that one should not forget when guiding one's friends or peers to guide oneself. Actually, more times than not, the deficiencies that we see in others can be found in ourselves as well, as we just witnessed with the king and his entourage.

EDUCATING CHILDREN AND SPEAKING THEIR LANGUAGE

PARSHAS EMOR

אֱמֹר אֶל הַכֹּהֲנִים, בְּנֵי אַהֲרֹן, וְאָמַרְתָּ אֲלֵהֶם (כא, א)

Say to the Kohanim, the children of Aharon, and say to them...

A dear friend of mine told me about the first day he went to Mountaindale Yeshiva:

As I stepped out of the car for the first time onto the Mountaindale Yeshiva campus, the Rosh Yeshiva, R. Rothenberg, waved me onto the basketball court and challenged me to a game. Being that I had my share of run-ins with many Roshei Yeshiva in the past and that I was a very tough sixteen-year-old teenager who knew how to play basketball, I felt delighted to show this rabbi a thing or two. To make a long story short, I lost the game. Afterwards, R. Rothenberg put his arm around me, and with a very warm smile said, "Welcome home, my dear Chaim Yehuda, it is a pleasure to have you aboard. I am looking

> forward to seeing you in the *Beis Medrash*." For the first time in my life I felt that the rabbi was speaking my language, and I indeed felt at home.[182]

Understanding our children is essential when it comes to education.[183] This includes their personality, abilities, talents, characteristics, intrinsic nature, as well as their age. Shlomo haMelech taught us to "teach a child according to whom he is."[184] If we do not know who they are, how can we begin to teach them?

This requires us to "figure them out" so that we can properly guide and shape them into the beautiful human beings that they are supposed to become. Working within a child's parameters makes the potential for the child to blossom that much greater.

R. Eliezer Friedman says that this extends to communication as well.[185] Sometimes one has to speak gently to a specific child and harshly to the next, elaborate to one and sharp to the next. It all depends on the audience.

Rashi explains an apparent redundancy at the beginning of our *parshah*. Why was Moshe told twice to tell the *kohanim* these laws of *tumah*? One time was not enough? Rashi explains that there were really two warnings. The initial warning was for the older *kohanim* and the second warning was to ensure that the older *kohanim* would also convey these laws to the younger *kohanim*, primarily their children.

This explains one redundancy. However, something else seems superfluous in this *parshah*. Why does the Torah write, "And [Moshe will] say to them [the *kohanim*]," when just four words earlier the Torah wrote explicitly that Moshe should tell the *kohanim*? Did we forget our audience?

The answer is that the Torah is teaching us, by adding the words "to them," that parents must address each child individually in a way that they can understand. "Say to them," implies in their language.

---

182 I heard this from the boy himself.

183 Look in *Alei Shor*, vol. 1, pgs. 262–263.

184 *Mishlei* 22:6, "*Chanoch le'naar al pi darko*."

185 From Montreal, Canada, in his *sefer Emunas Yirmiah*.

When an educator knows and understands this secret, he or she can then get in touch with the child, influence him, and lead him in the right direction.

How fortunate we are to have the Torah guiding us every step of the way.

May we see the fruits of our labors in our children and *talmidim* so that they too will walk in the ways of *Hashem*.

TRUSTING IN HASHEM

PARSHAS BEHAR

וְצִוִּיתִי אֶת בִּרְכָתִי (כה, יט–כא)
I will command My *brachah*.

The Alshich was teaching his *talmidim* about *bitachon*.[186] He said that one who completely trusts in Hashem will be taken care of. He will not need to work and will be able to devote his entire life to Torah and *tefillah*. A wagon driver was walking by and overheard the Alshich's *drashah*. He immediately took the Alshich's words to heart, sold his donkey and wagon to a non-Jew and started to recite *Tehillim* in the *shul*. Even though his family thought that he had gone mad, he continued to recite his *Tehillim* knowing that Hashem would take care of him.

After a few days, the donkey wandered back to the wagon driver's house carrying a treasure chest. It turned out that the non-Jew who bought it was a thief who planned to skip town with all his booty. He had accidentally slipped off the wagon while loading it with his treasure chest and died when hitting the floor. The donkey wandered back to the place that it knew — the wagon driver's home — and the wagon driver was left with enough treasures to devote his entire life to *avodas Hashem*.

186 Look in *Sichos Mussar* 5731, ch. 20.

The *talmidim* could not understand why the simple wagon driver was *zoche* to such a miracle and they were not. The Alshich explained it to them with a *mashal*: If you stick a knife into the ground and do not pull it out, it will stay securely in the ground forever. However, if you pull it out and then put it back in repeatedly, the ground will get soft and will not hold the knife. "The wagon driver stuck his trust into Hashem and did not pull it out," he told them, "whereas you, my dear *talmidim*, have put your trust into Hashem and pulled it out when things got tough. Your soil has already softened and does not hold as well."

"Trust completely in Hashem, my *talmidim*," continued the Alshich, "no matter what the case will be, and you too will be *zoche* to see Hashem's salvation, for as much as you trust in Him, that is how much He will be there for you.[187]

Chazal compare *bitachon* to a shadow. If you put two fingers into the sunlight, a two-finger shadow will appear; if you put your whole hand into the sunlight, then a shadow of a whole hand will appear. So too with *bitachon*: as much as we trust in Hashem, that is exactly how much Hashem will be there for us.

The Seforno explains that the two different *brachos* that Hashem gives to the *shomrei shvi'is* are dependent on their trust in Hashem. If they fully trusted in Hashem, then a third of what they would regularly eat during a non-*shemitah* year would satiate them on *shemitah*. Hence, one crop would be able to span over a period of three years.

However, those who also worried would receive a smaller *brachah*. Their crop would be blessed quantitatively, not qualitatively. It will produce in the sixth year a crop three times as much as the other years.

As a result, those who fully trusted in Hashem will have a peaceful year with plenty of time to devote to their *avodas Hashem*, whereas those who worried will have to work harder to compensate for their

---

187 Look in *Ha'maspik La'ha'oved Hashem* from Rav Avraham ben HaRambam, in *Sha'ar Habitachon*, pg. 82.

imperfect *bitachon*. They will have to spend their time tending to their exceptionally large crop and have much less time to devote towards their *avodas Hashem*.[188]

R. Eliyahu Lopian[189] writes that the *parshah* of *shemitah* is a lesson for life. The more we trust in Hashem, the more Hashem will be there for us.

---

188 This is how the *Seforno* reads *pesukim* 19–21: "If you keep the *shivi'is* year with a high level of trust, then you will receive a qualitative blessing. The land will produce its fruit and you will eat your fill. Even a small amount will satiate you as if you ate three times as much. However, if you show signs of doubtfulness and ask 'What will I eat?' then I will bless your produce quantitatively and the sixth year will produce three times the amount of produce more than the previous years. That way you will have enough for the seventh, eighth, and ninth years."

189 Look in *Lev Eliyahu* on this *pasuk* at length.

GIVING FOR THE SAKE OF GIVING

PARSHAS BEHAR

אַל תִּקַּח מֵאִתּוֹ נֶשֶׁךְ וְתַרְבִּית (כה, לו)
Do not take from him interest and increase.

My wife and I are in always in awe every *erev* Succos as we witness our *rabbanim* inspecting *lulavim* and *esrogim* at no cost, for hours on end. Nothing can describe those moments more than pure selflessness for the sake of the community.

The rabbis who make themselves available to their congregants 24/7 and the *askanim* who work around the clock to improve our society also score quite high on the purely selfless people list. Not to mention the countless people who have private *gemachim* in their homes. One amazing individual is R. Benny Fisher, who works at least eighteen hours a day offering free professional and exceptionally reliable medical advice to anyone. You can even call him at two in the morning.

The mitzvah of lending money without interest teaches us to do acts of kindness for others without asking "what is in it for me?" Not only is it forbidden to receive interest for lending money, but the person who borrowed the money is also not permitted to do any special favors for the person who lent him the money. That is even if both parties agree!

The Torah is telling us to lend money because of the desire to help another Jew, even though there is nothing in it for us. Develop your attribute of selfless giving.[190]

190 I heard this in the name of R. Chaim Shmuelevitz.

IT IS ALL FROM HASHEM

PARSHAS BECHUKOSAI

וְזָכַרְתִּי אֶת בְּרִיתִי יַעֲקֹב... לֹא מְאַסְתִּים (כו, מב)

I will remember my *bris* with Yaakov...nor will I have rejected them.

In the middle of the *Tochachah*, Hashem proclaims something that seems to be out of place. He says that His *bris* with Klal Yisroel is an everlasting one and that He will love and cherish them forever.[191] R. Yaakov Neiman asks, what is this doing right in the middle of the *Tochachah*?[192] When a father reprimands his child, does he discuss the love and affection that he has for him right in the middle?

R. Neiman writes that these *pesukim* symbolize the ray of hope amongst all the *Tochachah*. This ray of hope is there to give us the fortitude needed to weather the *Tochachah*.

He explains that on a superficial level, it may appear from all of the pain and suffering that Hashem has forgotten about Klal Yisroel. To that, Hashem responds: "even during the *Tochachah* you must know that I will never leave you. To demonstrate this, I am going to incorporate some goodness amongst all your pain and suffering. My

191 Based on Rashi, *pasuk* 44.
192 *Darchei Mussar, Parshas Bechukosai.*

dear *kinderlach*, learn from that goodness that even your pain and suffering is from Me and that I am still with you."

Yosef's journey down to Mitzrayim illustrates this perfectly. Even though the merchants traveling to Mitzrayim usually carried pitch and tar, the day Yosef traveled they "miraculously" carried wonderful smelling fragrances. Hashem arranged merchants carrying perfumes to be Yosef's chauffer.[193]

From here we see that ray of hope — Hashem's guided hand amongst all of Yosef's darkness and suffering. That goodness reminded Yosef that Hashem was with him every step of the way and taught him that all his suffering was in reality Hashem's goodness in disguise.

This is the ray of hope hiding within these *pesukim*, says R. Neiman. Hashem is telling Klal Yisroel in the middle of the *Tochachah*: "I will always remember you. I will send you some goodness within all the misfortune in order for you to realize that I am still with you and that your pain and suffering is from Me."[194]

This fundamental idea is true for Klal Yisroel as a whole and for every individual personally. If a person who is experiencing pain and suffering will open his eyes, he will find that his anguish is buffered by some goodness. It might be something seemingly insignificant like merchants carrying pleasant fragrances instead of pitch, but from there he can draw forth comfort and fortitude knowing that the pain and suffering is really Hashem's goodness in disguise and that Hashem never left his side. This will give him the strength needed to weather the suffering.

We all have our hardships that we have to weather. The key to survival is to find that goodness, that "I will always remember you" attached to the hardships, and to realize that those hardships are really Hashem's goodness in disguise and that He is with each and every one of us for eternity.

---

193 See Rashi on *Bereishis* 37:25.

194 These *pesukim* are so vital to us and our beliefs that Chazal decided to incorporate them into the *tefillos* of Rosh Hashanah.

SEFER BAMIDBAR

OUR CENTERPIECE

PARSHAS BAMIDBAR

וְנָסַע אֹהֶל מוֹעֵד, מַחֲנֵה הַלְוִיִּם, בְּתוֹךְ הַמַּחֲנֹת (ב, יז)

The *Ohel Mo'ed*, the camp of the *Levi'im*, shall journey in the center of the camps.

I ran into an old acquaintance of mine who hadn't seen me for many years. He was surprised to see how rich and meaningful my life had become. (Unfortunately, he did not choose a Torah lifestyle for himself). "Wow, you really figured yourself out, didn't you? You managed to build for yourself a happy and meaningful life," he commented. I remarked, "To tell you quite frankly, I didn't do anything. I just let the Torah guide my life and this is where it has led me."

There are so many books written today on every subject under the sun. Every few years, new theories and techniques are introduced and we are told to discard the old ones and try the newest and more improved ones. However, even with all the new theories, these books leave their customers dissatisfied, always searching for more. The Torah, however — the ultimate "bestseller" — has never and will never change,[195] and has within it the recipe for real happiness.

195 The fifth principal of faith: "*Zos haTorah lo tiheye moochlefes.*"

Anybody who will open up his heart to its wisdom will discover solutions for every situation. Its knowledge and guidance are what we so desperately need today to turn our life into a beautiful one.

The secret is to place the Torah in the center of our lives.

The Chafetz Chaim writes that our *bimahs* are in the center of our *shuls,* just as the *Eitz haChaim* [which is symbolic of the Torah] was planted in the center of *Gan Eden* and the *Aron haKodesh* was in the center of Klal Yisroel's encampment in the Midbar. All this is there to teach us that the Torah belongs in the center of our lives.

It is more than just a mere rulebook or something that one incorporates into one's life when convenient or beneficial; it is a way of life and this way of life contains the framework needed for a happy and meaningful life too. Contrary to popular opinion, it does not constrict our activities, but rather enhances our lives by giving us direction and purpose.[196] So much so, that the more a person makes the Torah the center of his life, the more he will discover its real inherent beauty.

As we approach Shavuos, we should remind ourselves of the wonderful gift that Hashem has given us. Sometimes, we may forget the beauty of the Torah and see it as a heavy burden, but in truth, it is a bag of diamonds whose weight one does not mind carrying. The more one makes an effort to fit himself and his life into the Torah, the more he will discover its splendor and the more precious it will be to him. We should learn from Klal Yisroel's encampment in the Midbar, our *bimahs* and the *Eitz haChaim*, as the Chafetz Chaim taught us, to make the Torah the core and center of our lives.

---

196 "Great is Torah that it gives life to the ones who do it." *Avos* 6:7.

EMULATING HASHEM

PARSHAS NASSO

וּמָחָה אֶל מֵי הַמָּרִים (ה,כג)
And erase it into the bitter waters.

The Medrash relates a story of a woman who delayed in coming home one Friday night due to her participation in Rebbi Meir's *drashah*.[197] By the time she arrived home, the Shabbos *licht* had extinguished and her husband was furious. She told him where she had been and he told her that she could not come into the house until she spat in Rebbi Meir's eye!

Eliyahu haNavi appeared to Rebbi Meir and told him what had happened. As soon as Rebbi Meir saw the woman reappear in the *Beis Medrash* he called her to his aid.[198] "Can you please help me? I have an eye ache and your spit would help alleviate my pain." He asked her to spit into his eye seven times and she did just that. Afterward, Rebbi Meir said to this woman, "Now go home and tell your husband that although he told you to spit into Rebbi Meir's eye once, you spat into his eye seven times!"

Rebbi Meir put his honor aside in order to bring *shalom bayis* between husband and wife. Amazing!

---

197 *Lev Eliyahu* brings this *Medrash* about Rebbi Meir. Rashi on *Avos* 1:12 also brings it regarding Aharon haKohen.

198 The Medrash says that she went to *daven*.

The *talmidim* asked Rebbi Meir in astonishment, "Rebbi, if you would have told us about such a man, we would have given him lashes and escorted his wife into her home. Why then did Rebbi completely disgrace himself by letting her spit into his eye seven times?"

Rebbi Meir told his *talmidim* that he learned such conduct from Hashem. "Do you think that my honor is greater than the honor of our Creator?" he asked them. "If Hashem is willing to erase His holy name in order to bring *shalom* between a suspected wife and her husband, when He could have accomplished the same thing without erasing His name, then most certainly I can do the same and have a wife spit in my face in order to bring *shalom bayis*."

Avraham Avinu also learned how to do *chessed* from Hashem.[199] He saw that Hashem's kindness is extremely lavish and that His giving is immeasurable. Hashem made a world filled with such diversity — there are hundreds of fruits and vegetables, thousands of colors, and so many different types of animals for us to enjoy. Avraham followed Hashem's example and gave without limit too.When the three wayfarers passed by his tent, for example, he slaughtered three cows so that each wayfarer would have a whole cow tongue to himself, even when one tongue could easily feed eight people.

As we can see, emulating Hashem goes far beyond bringing *shalom bayis* to husband and wife. The Gemara gives us many examples of how Hashem acted with kindness, compassion, and concern, and it is our obligation to emulate these actions.[200] Every time we take care of the poor, visit the sick, or have guests in our home, we are fulfilling the mitzvah of emulating Hashem.[201] Moreover, it makes us better people, makes the world a better place, and above all, brings us closer to Hashem.

---

199 Look in the *Sifsei Chaim, Middos v'Avodas Hashem,* vol. 1, pg. 283.

200 Hashem visited the sick, dressed the unclothed, and buried the dead etc. *Sotah* 14a. Look in *Sifsei Chaim, Middos v'Avodas Hashem*, vol. 1, pg. 273, in the name of R. Dessler.

201 The mitzvah is *"ve'halachta b'drachav"*; *Devorim* 28:8. It is good to think that you are doing this in order to fulfill Hashem's will of emulating Him.

LIVING IN UNITY

PARSHAS NASSO

וַיָּבִיאוּ אֶת קָרְבָּנָם...שֵׁשׁ עֶגְלֹת (ז, ג)

They brought up their *korbanos*...six wagons...a wagon for each two *Nesi'im*.

Yaakov Avinu's sprit was revived when he saw the wagons that Yosef had sent.[202] The *Daas Zakeinim* understands that they were symbolic of the six wagons that the *Nesi'im* contributed for the inauguration of the *Mishkan* at the end of our *parshah*.[203]

Their hope in sending only six wagons for twelve *shevatim* was to defuse any potential competitiveness that could have arisen during the inauguration ceremony. Since each *Nasi* had his chance to show his loyalty to Hashem during the inauguration, there was much room for jealousy and strife. By forcing them to share wagons, one wagon for two *shevatim*, they hoped to instill a sense of unity amongst themselves. They also standardized the day's *korban* with the hope that it would also neutralize any competitiveness created by each *Nasi* trying to outdo the other.

---

202 *Bereishis* 45:27.

203 The *Daas Zekeinim* on *Bereishis* ibid., as opposed to Rashi who understands that the wagons were symbolic of the *eglah arufah* that Yaakov and Yosef learned about before Yosef had disappeared.

Although Yaakov Avinu was relieved to hear that the hatred between his children had not cost Yosef his life, nonetheless he was still concerned that such hatred might rise again in the future and these wagons calmed that fear.[204] The wagons showed him that his children were not only aware of their differences and the potential strife that could come from them, but that they were also working in spite of those differences to unify themselves.

Today there are conflicts that arise in *shuls* and *Batei Medrashim* due to "politics" or personality clashes. We might not have wagons to share, but we can learn from the wagons of the *Nesi'im* that even in times of competition and pressure, we must stay unified.

Selfish thinking brings conflict.[205] Perhaps if we remind ourselves of the larger picture — Hashem's will — the conflicts will disappear and we will live in harmony once again.

---

204 Based on the writings of R. Yissocher Frand in *Rabbi Frand on the Parshah*.

205 Look in *Sha'arei Teshuva* 1:31.

THE VIRTUES OF HUMILITY

PARSHAS BEHA'ALOSCHA

וְהָאִישׁ מֹשֶׁה עָנָיו מְאֹד מִכֹּל הָאָדָם (יב, ג)

The man Moshe was exceedingly humble, more than any person on the face of the earth.

Somebody asked the Chafetz Chaim, "Why aren't people running after me like they are running after you? We are both *talmidei chachamim*!" The Chafetz Chaim empathized with him and then responded with the following: "Hashem told honor to run away from the people who are looking for it, and instead to run towards the people who are hiding from it. The reason why it is running after me and not you is because I have been running away from honor and you have been running after it."

"Good guys finish last" is a phrase that most of us have heard. Today's world believes that the people who do not stand up for themselves when being insulted or ridiculed will eventually be taken advantage of.[206] However, the Torah teaches us differently. The Vilna

206 This is not necessarily referring to a situation where one has a right to make a claim in *beis din*. Look in the end of the *Sifsei Chaim*, *Emunah v'Hashgacha* 1:13, what he writes in the name of R. Yisroel Salanter. There are certain

Gaon writes that Hashem gives a special shine[207] to the humble.[208] He writes that people who silently accept ridicule or insult become liked and beloved people.[209] This is evident by today's Torah leaders. They do not react to insult or run after fame and honor, yet people flock to them by the thousands.[210]

In our *parshah* we find an additional *brachah* that comes with humility. Moshe was silent when being criticized by Miriam and Aharon. This silence was not because Moshe was shy or apprehensive in any way. On the contrary, history has shown that Moshe was a man of confidence and poise. He confronted Pharaoh and reprimanded Klal Yisroel without hesitation, yet when it came to his own disgrace, he remained silent.

Although Moshe did not defend himself against their criticism, Hashem did. The Ramban explains that Hashem came to Moshe Rabbeinu's defense because Moshe was exceedingly humble.[211] Here we see an added dimension to humility. The more humble one is, the more Hashem will defend him when being criticized.

Humility is an attribute that brings one graciousness as well as the merit of Hashem's defense. Once a person knows and understands that accepting insult with silence invites Hashem's *brachah* into his life, he might actually find that accepting it is a bit more palatable. It could be that the only reason why the world says "good guys finish last" is because the world does not have Hashem in its equation. However, we who know the truth and view it daily with our Torah leaders understand and believe that "good guys" could actually come out ahead.[212]

---

situations where the Torah obligates and/or gives one right to claim damages or payments. There are other situations too where a person can have *ta'arumos* — complaints. However, outside of these situations, it is prohibited to have any complaints against another; instead one needs to turn towards Hashem.

207 A *Chen* — charm or grace.

208 Look at his commentary on *Mishlei* 3:34.

209 Look in *Chovos Halevavos, Sha'ar Hakenia*, ch. 10, "*Hashlishi...be'ma hiesa adon lechol benei dorecha.*"

210 Look in *Ohr Hachaim Hakadosh* at the end of *Parshas Ki Sisa.*

211 Look at the rest of the *pesukim*.

212 Look in *Chovos Halevavos, Sha'ar Hakenia*, ch. 5, where he lists many attributes that come from humility.

I Love Mitzvos

Parshas Beha'aloscha

וַיַּעַשׂ כֵּן אַהֲרֹן (ח, ג)
Aharon did so.

When Rabbeinu Tam was five years old, he saw his mother crying intently over the loss of her father, his *Zeide*, the great Torah giant Rashi. "Why are you crying so much?" he asked his mother. She answered him with these profound words, "Hashem just extinguished the light of the world." He looked into her eyes and said, "Don't worry, Mommy. I will make that light shine again."

The truth is that we all have the ability to illuminate the world with our Torah and mitzvos. This is what our mothers *daven* for every Friday night when they light the Shabbos *licht*: "Allow me to raise children...who will illuminate the world with Torah and good deeds and with every labor in the service of the Creator."

Aharon haKohen knew the preciousness of even one mitzvah and sought after it with all of his might. After Aharon lit the *Menorah,* he was praised for not deviating from Hashem's command.[213] The *Sefas Emes* explains that this praise cannot be understood literally,

213 According to Rashi.

Sefas Emes explains that this praise cannot be understood literally, because nobody would deviate from Hashem's direct command, all the more so Aharon. Rather the *pasuk* is praising Aharon's never-changing attitude towards mitzvos — they never became stale to him. Even a mitzvah that he had done thousands of times was greeted with the same fervor and enthusiasm that he had the first time he did it. Knowing this, we can understand why Aharon was so broken from witnessing all the *shevatim* participate in the inauguration of the *Mishkan* — that is, with the exception of his *shevet*. The mere fact that he and his *shevet* were not represented was to him a missed opportunity that pained him exceedingly. For such a thing to distress someone really shows where his priorities and concerns are.[214]

R. Avigdor Miller would advise people to say aloud that they love to do mitzvos while doing them. He would say that it would trigger real feelings of love for mitzvos. When you walk in your house, don't just kiss the *mezuzuah* and walk in. Rather kiss it and say aloud that you love mitzvos. When you are getting ready for Shabbos, let your whole family know that you love Shabbos.

Today many people can find within themselves an initial motivation that can propel them towards a mitzvah. However, more often than not, the motivation fades and is soon forgotten. So many people have passions for so many things. Let us learn from Aharon that we should channel our passions for the things that light up the world: our Torah and mitzvos.

---

214 This is very much connected to the first Rashi of our *parshah*, where he explains why *Parshas Beha'aloscha* follows *Parshas Nasso*.

Hashem's Mercy Is Boundless

Parshas Shelach

וַה' אִתָּנוּ אַל תִּירָאֻם (יד, ט)
Hashem is with us.

Mr. Newman left the doctor's office with a very discouraging diagnosis. The doctor gave him between six and twelve months to live. By the time he arrived at home and related the news to his wife, he was broken with despair. His wife on the other hand, responded optimistically. "I don't care what the doctor said; Hashem can do anything. I'll get my friends to say *Tehillim*, we will get *brachos* from the *Gedolim*, and *b'ezras Hashem* we will be *zoche* to a *yeshuah*."[215]

He replied with a sigh. "My dear wife, I believe in Hashem and I know that He can do whatever He wishes, but I don't believe that I am worthy enough to be a recipient of His compassion and kindness. I am not a *tzaddik* and I don't possess enough mitzvos that Hashem would want to make me part of the two percent that survive such a diagnosis."

215 Based on an essay found in *Facing Adversity with Faith* (Feldheim), pg. 99.

The *Chovos Halevavos* writes that a vital element in *bitachon* is to believe that Hashem's compassion and generosity holds no bounds.[216] Besides believing that everything that happens is for the good, one has to believe that Hashem bestows His kindness to the worthy and unworthy alike. The *Chovos Halevavos* writes further that this aspect of *bitachon* is so vital that without it, one's *bitachon* is not considered *bitachon*.

He explains that by definition, *bitachon* brings peace of mind and tranquility to the person who acquires it. On the contrary, a person who thinks that Hashem only bestows His generosity upon the deserving will always wonder whether or not he is worthy, as Mr. Newman did in our aforementioned story. Only a person who truly believes that Hashem gives to those who are not worthy and worthy alike will have such tranquility, and that is why this element is imperative to *bitachon*.

The Chafetz Chaim writes that Mr. Newman's mistake was similar to the mistake of the *Meraglim*.[217] The *Meraglim* did not doubt for a moment Hashem's might. They had just witnessed the greatest events of all time, including the *Eser Makkos* and *Kerias Yam Suf*. They knew that Hashem could wipe away all the nations that were in Eretz Yisroel within the blink of an eye. However, they did not believe that they were worthy of such a miracle. Why would Hashem save them? They were not *tzaddikim* who merited such salvation; after all, they had just committed the *Chet haEgel*.

This, says the Chafetz Chaim, is a big mistake. Hashem never made a condition with Klal Yisroel that He would only save the *tzaddikim*. Rather, anybody who does not blatantly rebel against Hashem or try to undermine His mitzvos can hope and anticipate that Hashem's goodness and salvation will come his way. This was what Yehoshua and Calev tried to tell Klal Yisroel when they said, "If we do not rebel against Hashem, then in turn, He will desire us and wipe away the nations that stand in our way; He is with us."[218]

216 *Chovos Halevavos, Sha'ar Habitachon*, ch. 1.

217 *Sh'miras Halashon*, 2:19.

218 14:8–9.

It is true that both the *Meraglim* and Mr. Newman recognized Hashem's might, but they mistakenly did not believe in Hashem's infinite compassion.[219] As a result, they lacked the peace and tranquility that accompanies *bitachon*. It is imperative for all of us to believe that Hashem bestows His kindness even to people who are unworthy. We should not be afraid or intimidated due to our stature, or think that worthiness is a credential when it comes to Hashem's infinite compassion. We too can *daven* for help and anticipate goodness, because Hashem's mercy is boundless.

219 When we speak of the *Meraglim* and their mistake, it must be taken with a grain of salt. They were on levels that we cannot even fathom. We are applying the episode of the *Meraglim* to our lives in order that we can learn and grow on our level.

ATTAINING YIRAS SHAMAYIM

PARSHAS SHELACH

וּרְאִיתֶם אֹתוֹ וּזְכַרְתֶּם אֶת כָּל מִצְוֹת (טו, לט)

And you shall see it and you shall remember all the mitzvos.

Many people have a misconception when it comes to *yiras Shamayim*. They feel that just as they fear burglars and mice, so too they should fear Hashem. As such, they attempt to jump-start or ignite their feelings of *yiras Shamayim*, but to their dismay, they never succeed. Their mistake is that they are looking for *yiras Shamayim* in a place where it does not exist. When Hashem created us, He purposely did not implant into us or our feelings any traces of *yiras Shamayim*.[220] Consequently, *yiras Shamayim* will never come naturally to us.[221]

If we want *yiras Shamayim*, we must begin and end intellectually, not emotionally. We begin by making ourselves knowledgeable

220 If we would naturally fear sin we would not have any free will. Look in R. Yitzchak Blazer's introduction to *Ohr Yisroel*. It is also brought in *Sifsei Chaim, Middos v'Avodas Hashem*, vol. 2, pg. 472.

221 Look in *Mesilas Yesharim* at the end of ch. 25. Perhaps one day a person's *yiras Shamayim* that he has intellectually attained can drip into his emotions, but that is with much time and effort.

about it, that is by learning about reward and punishment and that Hashem sees, knows, and records everything we do. It is important to note, as mentioned above, that this knowledge will never influence us to do good, as it is only knowledge and will never affect us on an emotional level.

After accumulating some essential facts about *yiras Shamayim*, one can begin to choose to live with it, which for most of us is easier said than done. On our own, in spite of our desires and wants, we must actively decide to live in accordance with our knowledge.

This is particularly difficult for us because it requires battling our *yetzer hara* head on, and although he does not mind if we amass knowledge about *yiras Shamayim*, he does mind if we live with it. In retaliation, he sends out his emissaries — our desires and wants[222] — to counterattack and drown out any intellectually based *yiras Shamayim* that we have amassed. What makes it even more difficult to live with *yiras Shamayim* is the pressure that we feel from our desires and wants, as they are extremely influential when it comes to making decisions.[223]

In conclusion, *yiras Shamayim* is a decision we ourselves must make and no feeling or emotion will ever steer us to the side of good in that decision making.[224]

Tzitzis are known for their great ability to stop us from sinning. However, the actual *tzitzis* strings alone do not magically do this. They need introspection as well.[225]

---

222 Our wants and cravings have the power to drown out and smother what is ultimately right. Another example might be of a person who has an eating disorder or an alcohol addiction. No matter how much we reason with him, he will not stop eating and drinking, even if it is a matter of life or death.

223 This is what we call a bias. They are constantly fighting to drown out the *yiras Shamayim* that we have created for ourselves. Look in *Chovos Halevavos, Sha'ar Prishus*, ch. 2.

224 In truth, the *yetzer hara* only looks very powerful. The *Chovos Halevavos* in the beginning of *Sha'ar Yichud Hamaysa*, ch. 5, writes that just as a little bit of light can push away a lot of darkness, so too a little bit of truth can push away much falsehood. All of the *yetzer hara*'s tactics are based on lies and falsehood. If a person truly wants to fight him, the best ammunition is truth. It will pull the rug right out from underneath his feet.

225 "Do not follow the desires of your heart and eyes."

Chazal tell us that the blue of the *tzitzis*, the *techeles*, is there to remind us of the *Kisei haKavod*,[226] as well as the oceans and skies — Hashem's handiworks. With a little thought, a person can remind himself that the Creator of the Heavens and Earth is sitting on His heavenly throne watching and recording every move we make.

Intellectually speaking, such a thought should stop a person from giving into his desires, however, practically speaking, our emotions speak a different language.

That being the case, a person still has to make the executive decision and decide to listen to his intellect and put the reins on his desires.

In a similar vein, the *tzitzis* remind us to tie down our bodily desires and channel them towards *avodas Hashem*, just as we tie our garment with the *tzitzis* strings.[227]

R. Chaim Friedlander brings out another dimension regarding *tzitzis*.[228] Every soldier in the army has his badge. A private, a general, a five-star general etc. Our *tzitzis* is the Jew's badge, and this badge testifies that we are serving a higher source. May we wear our badge with pride.

---

226 Hashem's throne of glory.
227 Heard from R. Yitzchak Berkowitz, Rosh Kollel, Linas HaTzedek.
228 *Sifsei Chaim, Middos v'Avodas Hashem*, vol. 2, pg. 475.

YOU ARE SPECIAL BECAUSE YOU ARE YOU

PARSHAS KORACH

וַיִּקַּח קֹרַח (טז, א)
Korach separated himself.

From time to time, Dovid Engel would leave little notes of encouragement for his children around the house. One day, his daughter Esti found the following note on the breakfast table:

> My dear children, how I wish I could show you how beautiful each and every one of you are. You do not have to find shortcomings in others to make yourself shine. Miri, your smile can brighten up the world; Esti, your charm can win anybody's heart over; Naftali, your innate nature to organize can put tens of disorganized organizations back on their feet; Dovid, your power of adventure can make anything enjoyable; and Shimi, your internal happiness can carry you through any storm.
>
> Don't lose sight of your preciousness by placing your eyes onto somebody else's lot. You are bound to see talents,

blessings, and characteristics in your peers that you do not have. This is because you are you, and they are they. Each person was created with his or her talents and abilities to fulfill his role in life. Do not let your jealously blind you from seeing your own beauty and destroy your own world at the same time. It is debilitating.

Korach's jealously is what brought him to foolishly challenge Moshe and Aharon, and eventually mock the Torah. He never found happiness because of his jealousy—just disappointment and frustration. Moreover, all of his energies were to make Moshe inferior and not to make himself the person that he was supposed to be.

Your treasure is right in your own backyard. Don't let the fear of your unknown or potential faults frighten you away. Place your energies in your talents and your good character traits, and eventually you will become a beautiful person.[229]

Shlomo haMelech taught us that jealously rots our bones. It steals our happiness, turns our life into a constant disappointment, as well as blinds us from seeing the good that we truly possess.

Love, Tatty

229 Look in *Alei Shor*, vol. 1, pgs. 35–37.

BE HAPPY WITH YOUR LOT, IT IS HEAVEN SENT

PARSHAS KORACH

וּמַדּוּעַ תִּתְנַשְּׂאוּ עַל קְהַל ה׳ (טז, א)

Why do you exalt yourselves over the congregation of Hashem?

Yossi Klein had enough of his Rosh Yeshiva, his Gemara *rebbi*, and the *bochurim* of the yeshiva as well. He told his *mashgiach* that he was leaving the yeshiva with all of its problems and moving to another yeshiva where he would finally be able to find that peace and tranquility that he had been seeking. The *mashgiach* gently put his hand onto Yossi's shoulder and told him that if he really wanted to leave all of his problems behind, he should make sure to leave himself behind too. Otherwise, he would be bringing his problems with him to his new yeshiva.

Yaakov Hartman, as opposed to Yossi, had asked the *mashgiach* to change his *chavrusa* countless times, but to his disappointment, there was nobody else available. Instead of writing the situation off, Yaakov applied himself to the situation and finished the year with "the worst *chavrusa* in the world."

As the year progressed, so did Yaakov. He quickly learned how to keep his *chavrusa* interested with cakes and candies, speaking briefly, and building up everything that his *chavrusa* would say. After the year was over, Yaakov realized that he was not just surviving through a difficult *chavrusa*, but he was unearthing potentials in himself that would have otherwise lain dormant.

Thanks to the world's worst *chavrusa*, Yaakov become more patient with others, was able to explain things in a clearer fashion, and generally understand other people in ways that he never understood before. What seemed at first to be a nightmare turned out to be a wonderful *brachah* in disguise.

Korach never came to terms with who he was and the situation that he found himself in. He constantly fought the life that Hashem had tailor-made for him. As a result, his life was one of unease, frustration, and instability. A life void of peace of mind.

In contrast to Korach, Yosef haTzaddik was a person who found comfort, satisfaction, stability, and peace of mind in every situation that he found himself in. His brothers threw him into a pit and then sold him to wayfarers. One wayfarer sold him to the next until he finally reached Mitzrayim. There, he labored doing menial tasks as a slave, far from his dear father, family, and friends until he finally ended up in jail for twelve years for a crime that he did not even commit. Never once did he complain or resent his situation; on the contrary, he used it as a tool in his service of Hashem.

His secret was *emunah* in Hashem's *hashgachah pratis*. It allowed him to believe that everything that was happening to him was "Heaven sent." This gave him a sense of peace and tranquility that enabled him to serve Hashem even under the most difficult and extreme conditions.

It is imperative for a Jew to know and believe that Hashem is providing him with exactly what he needs in order for him to fulfill his role in this world.[230] Some people need a small family, others a larger one; some need poverty, while others riches. Whatever it might be, Hashem has set the stage for him to fulfill his role here on earth. The

---

230 Look in the *Seforno* at the end of *Parshas Tazria*; and in *Derech Hashem* 2:4:8–9.

Jew's job is not to wish the surroundings would be different,[231] but to work within the parameters that he was given and serve Hashem as best as he can.

Don't disregard or dismiss your situation; see it as Heaven sent and use it to the fullest.

People are always looking for the city of peace, but little do they know that it is found in the state of mind.

231 Of course we are supposed to *daven* to Hashem and ask Him to make the situation better, but in the meantime, if nothing changes, we have to know what to do.

A PRICELESS BRACHAH TEFILLAH

PARSHAS CHUKAS

וַנִּצְעַק אֶל ה' וַיִּשְׁמַע קֹלֵנוּ... וַיֹּצִאֵנוּ מִמִּצְרָיִם (כ, טז)
And Hashem heard our cries.

It was *leil* Shavuos, and Shimshon Pincus's father was heading off to *shul* to learn for the night. Although Shimshon very much wanted to go with him, his father had other plans. "I am sorry, my dear Shimshon," his father said as he kissed him goodbye, "but you are only six years old and are still too young to stay up the whole night." Shimshon walked his father to the door, said goodbye, and strangely enough just stood by the door, almost as if he was waiting for his father to come home.

Ten, fifteen, twenty minutes passed and he still was standing there waiting. "Shimshon, Tatty said that you are still too young to go with him this year," his mother called out. "Come sit on the couch and we'll read a book together." Shimshon did not budge until the front door opened and in came Shimshon's father. "What happened?" they asked.

"I changed my mind and decided to take Shimshon after all," answered Shimshon's father. "But why are you still standing by the door, Shimshon?"

The young Shimshon replied, "I told Hashem how much I wanted to go with you to *shul* and asked Him to bring you back. I was just waiting for you to come and take me."

We all possess this priceless *brachah* of *tefillah*; just some of us realize it sooner than others, and some of us believe in it sooner than others.

When Klal Yisroel requested permission to pass through Edom's land, Moshe warned and reminded Edom of this *brachah*. "When we cried out to Hashem in Mitzrayim, He saved us by punishing the *Mitzrim*. Edom, be careful not to harm us because if you do, we will cry out to Hashem and He will punish you just as He punished them."[232]

Moshe was referring to Klal Yisroel's *brachah* of *tefillah*, "*Hakol kol Yaakov*" that Yaakov Avinu had received from Yitzchok Avinu many years prior.[233] Rashi explains that this *brachah* was an eternal *brachah* to all of Klal Yisroel. Anytime a Jew sincerely cries out to Hashem, He will answer his call.[234]

The Steipler writes that even if many days or even years have passed and one feels that all of his *tefillos* have not helped, he should by no means stop *davening*. Neither should he despair, nor think for a moment that his *tefillos* were for naught, because no *tefillah* goes unanswered.[235] Chazal tell us that some *tefillos* help immediately, some after three days, and some after thirty or seventy years. Even though it may appear to us at times as if our *tefillos* were not heard, it is not true at all.[236]

Perhaps Hashem is saving those *tefillos* for a time when we would not be able to *daven*. As we saw,[237] R. Shimshon Pincus relates the story of a boy by the name of Eliyahu who *davened* for a sick friend

---

232 Look in *Be'ir Besadei*, a commentary on Rashi.

233 *Bereishis* 27:22. Look in *Sefer Hazikaron's* commentary on Rashi, where Rashi saw this in the *pasuk*.

234 Look in *She'arim B'tefillah, Tza'aka*.

235 *Chayai Olam*, ch. 28.

236 We have no concept of the ramifications of our *tefillos* and how much worse the situation would have been had we not have *davened*.

237 See *Parshas Vayeira*.

of his who unfortunately did not survive. R. Pincus explains that Hashem saved those *tefillos* and used them three months later when Eliyahu's brother, Yossi, was hit by a car. Unfortunately, Eliyahu did not hear about the accident until after Yossi's operation was a success. Little did Eliyahu know that it was in the merit of his *tefillos* that his younger brother was saved. Hashem heard his *tefillos*, saved them, and answered them just a few years later.[238]

Our lives are filled with *brachah* from morning to night. Unfortunately, routine can rob us from appreciating many of them. The power of *tefillah* is one of those eternal *brachos* that we are fortunate to have. We are supposed to pour our hearts out to Hashem and He will channel our *tefillos* in the right direction.

238 *She'arim B'tefillah, Eitor* 6.

PEACE OF MIND

PARSHAS CHUKAS

וַיִּבְכּוּ אֶת אַהֲרֹן שְׁלֹשִׁים יוֹם כֹּל בֵּית יִשְׂרָאֵל (כ, כט)

All the Jewish people cried for Aharon for thirty days.

Chazal tell us that Aharon haKohen was a lover and pursuer of peace. His pursuit extended to every facet of life, including other people's quarrels.

If he saw two people fighting, he would discretely approach one of them and say, "Your friend is broken and misses your friendship immensely. He desperately wants to make amends." Then he would say the same thing to the other friend and eventually reunite them.

Once he heard a husband say to his wife, "I will not speak to you until you spit into the eye of the *Kohen Gadol*." Aharon was such a pursuer of peace that he was even willing to disgrace himself for it. Aharon ran to the woman and pleaded for her help. "Can you please spit in my eye? I am suffering from a very painful eye infection that only the spit of a woman can cure."[239]

It is no wonder that Chazal say that there were over 80,000 children at Aharon haKohen's funeral bearing his name![240] Just imagine

239 Based on Rashi's commentary on *Avos* 1:12. See above, *Parshas Nasso*, "Emulating Hashem."

240 This is found in the *Pesikta Zuta*. All the families that he managed to touch in

how many countless hours he must have spent discussing *shalom bayis* issues with so many husbands and wives for so many of them to name their children in his honor.[241]

We are required to follow his example and become a pursuer of peace too.[242] The question is how. Are we also supposed to stick our head into other people's disputes and bring about reconciliation, or disgrace ourselves in order to bring about *shalom bayis*? For most of us, such requests are beyond our present capabilities.[243]

Perhaps we can suggest a non-conventional manner of how we can follow his example. While he sought after the "greater" peace, we can pursue a more specific peace: other people's "peace of mind."

I recall the first time one of our children had an extremely high fever. We were a young couple living in Eretz Yisroel with all of our relatives abroad. We were not able to call them in America for help, as it was one o'clock in the morning on *motzaei* Shabbos and it was still Shabbos for them. We were stuck with nobody to turn to. I noticed the Goldman's lights were still on; I called them, and *baruch Hashem* they helped us. They gave us something wonderful — peace of mind at one in the morning.

We all have our similar stress-related situations that sting us with anxiety and tension, like running out of baby diapers at two in the morning, or wanting to mail a letter and not having enough postage. Have you ever been too busy to pick up an important ingredient at the grocery store or forget to send in a recorder into a lecture that you so desperately wanted to hear?

Many people have learned from such stress-related experiences

---

his lifetime honored him by naming their children after him. Aharon haKohen passed away on *Rosh Chodesh* Av, during the fortieth year of Klal Yisroel's wandering in the Midbar, at the age of one hundred and twenty-three.

241 The Torah tells us that all the Jewish people cried for thirty days after his passing. If we translate the *pasuk* literally, it reads, "All of Klal Yisroel cried 'Aharon' for thirty days." Perhaps we can say that he made such an impression that they could not stop from crying "Aharon, Aharon" repeatedly. The "all" implies the men, women, and children alike because they were all affected.

242 Look in *Avos* 1:12, "*Havei m'talmidav shel Aharon haKohen*," and Rashi there.

243 However, there are definitely times where we too can intervene and bring *shalom* using Aharon haKohen's tactics.

how to help others. In Jewish communities around the world, people have opened up *gemachim* in their homes to lend out all sorts of things: medicines, medical equipment, baby formula, diapers, free loans, and even stamps. These *gemachim* are really offering peace of mind to those in need of it, and as such, following Aharon's example.

A twenty-four-hour diaper *gemach* can most definitely bring about some peace of mind. A stamp *gemach*, too, can calm a person who had to mail a letter already yesterday but could not find a stamp. There are even *gemachim* today that will pick up a package or run an errand for you when you are in a pickle.

There is a family in our neighborhood that is in charge of delivering cakes to every new family that moves into the neighborhood. Many newcomers are anxious about stepping into a new neighborhood. Will they be accepted into the community, will they fit in? Somehow, a cake manages to calm their nerves and bring them that peace of mind that they were looking for. Perhaps we could say that this family is also following Aharon's example of pursuing peace on a smaller scale — the peace of mind of others.

Becoming a student of Aharon is a lifetime project. There are unlimited ways to pursue peace. Let us embark together, today, on our journey towards making this world a world of peace, by bringing peace of mind to our friends, family, and neighbors.

DIGNITY AT ITS FINEST

PARSHAS BALAK

וַיִּפְתַּח יְהֹוָה אֶת פִּי הָאָתוֹן וַתֹּאמֶר (כב, כח)

Hashem opened the mouth of the donkey and it said.

R. Yechiel Mordechai Gordon, the late Rosh Yeshiva of the Lumze Yeshiva, relayed a story of an esteemed bochur in his yeshiva who had requested permission to speak at his own vort.

Towards the end of his *d'var Torah*, the *chasan* thanked Hashem, his parents, his Rosh Yeshiva, and *rebbeim*. He made a point of giving a particularly warm thank you to his second-grade *rebbi*.

The audience wondered what was so special about his second-grade *rebbi* to be singled out. The *chasan* explained: "If it wouldn't have been for my second-grade *rebbi*, I don't know if I would be a *ben Torah* today." He then related the following story of what happened to him when he was in second grade:

> One of my rich classmates brought a gold watch to class. Everybody was very jealous. The boy stepped out and left his watch on the table and I could not resist but take it! When the boy returned, he began screaming that his watch was stolen! The *rebbi* immediately commanded the entire

class to raise their hands as he checked all of our pockets.

When it came to my turn, I was shaking from fear, for I had the watch in my pocket. He found it, quickly slipped it into his sleeve, and continued checking everybody else's pockets without saying a word. When he returned to the front of the class, he announced, "I found the watch in one of the boy's pockets. He is a good boy; he was just not able to win over his *yetzer hara* today. I hope that in the future when his *yetzer hara* confronts him, he will be able to win."

The *chasan* concluded by saying, "Now you know why I am so thankful to my second-grade *rebbi*. If he had reacted differently and called me a thief, it would have been my end. I would not have been able find my place with my friends due to the sheer embarrassment and I would have taken a different course in life. Only in the merit of his conduct was he able to save me from destruction. He pitied my honor and I am forever grateful to him."

Let us think twice before we do something that might embarrass somebody. Who knows — maybe we can even turn the event full-circle and pick him up instead!

The Medrash says that Hashem killed Bilaam's donkey in order to spare Bilaam the mockery and ridicule that would have resulted if it had been alive. People would have seen the speaking donkey that reprimanded Bilaam and remarked, "Look, there is the donkey that reprimanded Bilaam."[244]

Hashem took pity on one of the most wicked, egocentric, and greedy people who ever lived, Bilaam haRasha. Astonishing! What is more amazing is that this speaking donkey would have made such a *kiddush Hashem* and still Hashem killed it in order to prevent shame and embarrassment to Bilaam.[245]

R. Chaim Shmuelevitz explains that the Torah is teaching us a level of sensitivity that we might not have thought of ourselves. No mat-

244 Rashi brings the *Medrash Tanchuma* on his commentary to 22:33.

245 The world would have seen Hashem's awesome handiwork in action, i.e., the speaking donkey.

ter how low or evil a person is, he is still a human being, and does not need to suffer embarrassment more than he deserves.[246]

If Hashem pities the dignity of the wicked, then we can surely find within ourselves the wherewithal to save our friends, children, and spouses from any embarrassment or shame that we might have thought to cause them.

246 Based on the *Sichos Mussar* 5733, 20.

PATIENCE

PARSHAS BALAK

וַיִּפְתַּח יְהוָה אֶת פִּי הָאָתוֹן וַתֹּאמֶר (כב, כח)

Hashem opened the mouth of the donkey and it said.

Hashem created a speaking donkey[247] in the hope that it would influence one of the most egocentric and corrupt individuals that ever lived, Bilaam haRasha, to do *teshuvah*, because He never gives up on anybody, even on Bilaam haRasha.[248]

Now, if Hashem is patient for someone as evil as Bilaam, then He is certainly patient with us. It has been over two thousand years and the Beis Hamikdash is still not rebuilt, and we are the culprits. Nonetheless, Hashem is still by our side, waiting for us to return to Him.

Rabbi Preida had to teach a certain *talmid* four hundred times before he was able to grasp the material. Once, even four hundred times was not enough!

---

247 *Avos* 5:2.

248 R. Chaim Shmuelevitz understands that this supernatural donkey was not created to save Klal Yisroel from Bilaam's curses, because if it was, it did a poor job doing so. Even after it spoke with Bilaam, he still continued to try to curse us. Its sole purpose of being created, says R. Chaim Shmuelevitz, was to stop Bilaam haRasha from sinning.

In the midst of their studies, there was a knock on the door requesting Rabbi Preida's presence. That knock affected the *talmid*'s ability to concentrate and instead of taking four hundred times for him to grasp the information, it took him eight hundred times. Rabbi Preida's level of patience was identical the eight hundredth time as it was the first time.[249]

Love, support, and respect, amongst many other virtuous attributes, all stem from patience. It does not matter if one is a teacher, parent, boss, worker, or just a friend, these attributes are all imperative for success.

Don't forget to be patient with yourself; it takes time to attain good *middos*. In the end, you will see that it is well worth its weight in gold.[250]

---

249 *Eruvin* 54b.

250 Look in *Alei Shor*, vol. 2, pgs. 213–224.

Appreciating What Hashem Does for Us

Parshas Balak

כִּי הֶעֱלִתִיךָ מֵאֶרֶץ מִצְרַיִם... עַמִּי זְכָר נָא מַה יָּעַץ בָּלָק (מההפטרה)

When I brought you up from the land of Mitzrayim and redeemed you...O' My people, remember now what Balak...plotted and what Bilaam...answered...that you know the righteous acts of Hashem.

In the *haftorah*, the *navi* Micha awakened feelings of gratitude and appreciation in Klal Yisroel by mentioning *Yetzias Mitzrayim* and the time Hashem saved Klal Yisroel from Bilaam's curse. We can all understand why the *navi* chose *Yetzias Mitzrayim* as a vehicle to awaken such feelings of gratitude. Hashem changed all the laws of nature to bring about our salvation. The blood, the frogs, the hail, the darkness, and the Splitting of the Sea are just a few examples of the hundreds, if not thousands, of miracles that He did for us. However, why did Micha mention the time Hashem foiled Bilaam's plans? What did Micha find so extraordinary in Hashem saving us from Bilaam's curse that it should engender these feelings of gratitude even more than the salvation from the hundreds of people that try to kill and curse us daily?[251]

251 Look in the Pesach Haggadah, *"Ve'he sheamda..."*

R. Simcha Ziskind Brody, the late Rosh Yeshiva of Yeshivas Chevron, gives us the answer.[252] He explains that the miracles of Mitzrayim were by far the greatest miracles that ever took place. Hashem changed the face of nature in front of our eyes. However, the miracle of foiling Bilaam's plan had an aspect that made it even more miraculous than all the miracles of Mitzrayim. The miracles of Mitzrayim existed within the physical world, whereas interfering with Bilaam's curse existed within the spiritual worlds.

Chazal tell us that Hashem incorporated into His master plan a moment in the day when He is angered.[253] This "moment" is found very high up in the spiritual worlds. Bilaam prided himself in knowing when that time was and had planned to utilize that moment to curse Klal Yisroel. Chazal tell us that he would have succeeded if Hashem would have actually been angered at those times. However, to his dismay, Hashem foiled his plans by "changing" His master plan and was miraculously not angered.[254]

"What can I do?" cried Bilaam to Balak. "G-d did not get angry when He was supposed to."[255] This change immobilized Bilaam and saved Klal Yisroel. Being that this miracle took place on a higher realm, it excelled, in that aspect, above and beyond all the other miracles that transpired in Mitzrayim.

Micha reminded Klal Yisroel of Hashem's kindness towards them,[256] hoping that it would awaken inside of them feelings of gratitude and appreciation. Such feelings should have ignited within them the internal will to give thanks to Hashem and reciprocate.

So too, on a personal level, noticing Hashem's kindnesses and generosities can bring a person to ask himself: Since Hashem has done so much for me, how can I reciprocate? Aside for *bircas Modim*,

---

252 Look in *Saam Derech*.

253 *Brachos* 7a.

254 *Saam Derech*.

255 Look in Rashi on *Bamidbar* 23:8.

256 Look in *Micha* there, "*L'man daas tzidkas Hashem*."

which allows a person to say thank you to Hashem daily, one can also reciprocate with action by fulfilling His will. According to Micha at the end of our *haftorah,*[257] fulfilling Hashem's will is done through justice, loving-kindness, and walking humbly with Hashem.

257 *"Kei im asos mishpat v'ahavas chessed v'hatzne leches im Elokecha."*

LIVING ABOVE THE STATISTICS

PARSHAS PINCHAS

אֵלֶּה בְנֵי בִנְיָמִן... אֵלֶּה בְנֵי דָן... (כו, מא–מב)

These are the sons of Binyomin.... These are the sons of Dan...

Many people can have all the requirements needed to succeed and still be unsuccessful. At the same time, many people can "lack it all" and flourish with success. The explanation is that statistics do not determine one's success and destiny; Hashem does.

In spite of Binyomin's ten children, his *shevet* only totaled 45,600 in Klal Yisroel's second census.[258] Dan, on the other hand, only had one deaf child, Chushim, and his *shevet* managed to total 64,400 in the poll. That means Dan's one deaf child produced over one-third more than Binyamin's ten healthy children did! How can that be?

The answer, says the Chafetz Chaim, is that statistics do not make

258 A sizeable portion of *Parshas Pinchas* is dedicated to Klal Yisroel's second census. Rashi explains that Hashem requested this census because last week's *parshah* ended with a plague that annihilated twenty-four thousand people from Klal Yisroel. Hashem therefore wanted to count His children who survived, just as a shepherd wants to count his flock after it has been ravaged by wolves.

the decisions; Hashem does. "Statistically" speaking, Binyomin's *shevet* should have been ten times larger than that of Dan. However, Hashem's infinite wisdom decided differently.[259]

R. Samson Rephael Hirsch explains similarly the *pasuk* of *"Pose'ach es yadecha, u'masbia le'kol chai ratzon."*[260] He translates the word *ratzon* to mean "charm and favor," and therefore translates the *pasuk* as follows: "Hashem, you open up your hands and satisfy every being with charm," meaning to say that Hashem gives us the charm needed to succeed and flourish in all of our endeavors.

When we want to be accepted into a community or a group of friends, or we want our businesses to prosper, it all boils down to one thing: how much charm and favor is Hashem going to grace us with. Again, we see that Hashem is in charge of our success. He is satisfying people, i.e., helping them make a *parnasah* by gracing them constantly with *ratzon* — the "charm" needed to succeed.

It is known that everybody used to flock to the Chafetz Chaim's store. So much so that he limited his store hours to the early morning in fear that he was taking away business from the other merchants. When he saw that it did not deter the customers, he limited his hours even more and when he realized that even that did not help, he eventually closed his store.

What made everybody run to the Chafetz Chaim's store and not to everybody else's stores? The Chafetz Chaim was the epitome of an *eved Hashem* and most probably due to his dedication to Hashem, he was graced with a charm that made him loved and respected by all.

The avenue of success is not through flattery or bribery; rather it is through fulfilling Hashem's will. The more one grows spiritually, the more Hashem will constantly bestow upon him a charm that will in turn allow him to succeed in his endeavors.

---

259 Based on the *Chafetz Chaim* on the Torah.

260 *Tehillim* 115:18, literally translated: "Hashem, You open up Your hands and satisfy every being with *ratzon*." The *pasuk* is usually understood to mean that either Hashem will satisfy everybody's wishes by giving them what they want or that Hashem will satisfy everybody in accordance with what Hashem wishes. However, R. Hirsch has a novel way of explaining the *pasuk*.

REINSTATING JUSTICE

PARSHAS MATTOS

נִקְמַת ה׳ בְּמִדְיָן (לא, ג)
Hashem's vengeance against Midian.

Hashem took vengeance against the Midianites after they enticed Klal Yisroel to sin and caused them to lose twenty-four thousand people to a plague.[261] Although vengeance usually has a negative connotation, when we speak of Hashem's vengeance, we are referring to reinstating Godliness in the world, which is not negative in the slightest; on the contrary, nothing could be more beautiful.[262]

Sin, in and of itself, is a *chillul Hashem*. It shows that a person can defy Hashem's will. Sin without consequences is even a greater *chillul Hashem* because it shows that people can sin and get away with it too. Therefore, when Hashem avenged Midian, a *kiddush Hashem* was created because He taught the world that there is indeed justice.[263]

---

261 Look at the end of last week's *parshah*. Obviously, Klal Yisroel had the free will not to sin; however, Midian was punished for enticing them.

262 This week's *d'var Torah* is based on the writing of R. Betzalel Rakov, the Gateshead Rav.

263 In this light, we can view the plague that killed twenty-four thousand Jews as a *kiddush Hashem* as well.

"*Nikmas Hashem b'Midian*—Hashem's vengeance against Midian,"[264] implies that the war was solely for Hashem's honor and justice. Human revenge is unjustified and even prohibited by the Torah.[265] However, reinstating Hashem's honor is a tremendous mitzvah.

Vengeance, like all attributes is essentially neutral. It just depends on where and why it is being used. In our Western culture, few people, if any, know what is truly right and wrong, let alone know when to take a stand and when to back down. Lucky are we who have the Torah, the ultimate truth, to guide our every action. It even teaches us when vengeance is appropriate. To be able to know the ultimate truth is one of the biggest, if not the biggest, gift that Hashem has given us. Let us cherish it.

---

264 31:3.

265 That is, revenge for one's honor and pride.

PRIORITIZING

PARSHAS MATTOS

אַחַר תֵּאָסֵף אֶל עַמֶּיךָ (לא, א)

Afterward you will be brought in unto your people.

Moshe Rabbeinu was commanded to wage war against Midian, but, Hashem never told him when to begin. Regardless of the fact that Hashem also told Moshe that he would die immediately after the war, he began it as soon as he could.[266]

Can you imagine? Moshe's death was dependent on the war and instead of procrastinating, he ran to begin it!

The Chiddushei haRim explains that Moshe's entire essence was for *kavod Shamayim*, and since *kavod Shamayim* was going to emanate from the war with Midian, Moshe ran to do it as quickly as possible. For Moshe, it was another opportunity to honor Hashem. Nothing more needed to be said because everything else, even his life, paled in comparison.

Although we are not on the level of Moshe, we can still make Hashem's honor the priority of our lives. Such a goal can refocus many seemingly difficult situations.

---

266 *Medrash Tanchuma, Mattos* 3.

Consider the following example: You are in line and somebody cuts you off. If your ego is the priority of your life, then feelings of being insulted might rise to the surface. However, if Hashem's honor is the focus, we would react in a pleasant manner, making sure that a *kiddush Hashem* would be made.

Yes, it entails a refocusing of priories to live for Hashem, but it is something that is reachable to all of us. Perhaps the solution for such a situation would be to refocus by asking ourselves what does Hashem want from me at this moment, and then doing it.

Furthermore, if we are to take a step back and remind ourselves that Hashem is the One who has placed us in our present predicament, it will be easier not to insult the person who cut us off or to get upset at him, rather to make our own personal *kiddush Hashem*.[267]

---

267 Look in *Michtav M'Eliyahu*, vol. 1, pg. 22; *Chovos Halevavos, Sha'ar Habitachon*, ch. 3, introduction 5.

THE GIFT OF LIFE

PARSHAS MATTOS

וְאֵת בִּלְעָם בֶּן בְּעוֹר הָרְגוּ בֶּחָרֶב (לא, ח)

And Bilaam son of Beor, they killed with the sword.

R. Naftoli Trop, the late Rosh Yeshiva of Radin, was critically ill. The *talmidim* were very concerned and wanted to help. Suddenly, one of the *talmidim* got up and announced that he would donate one year of his life to the Radiner Rosh Yeshiva, R. Naftoli Trop. Another *talmid* then volunteered two years, and then another three. As the air filled with enthusiasm to save their Rosh Yeshiva, they thought it would be appropriate to visit the great Chafetz Chaim and ask him to contribute as well. How much would the Chafetz Chaim give to R. Naftoli they wondered? A year, two, or maybe even three?

When they arrived and asked the Chafetz Chaim, he thought for a moment and told them these words: "I will give two minutes of my life for the great Radiner Rosh Yeshiva."

The *talmidim* left the Chafetz Chaim shocked and disheartened. The Chafetz Chaim's love for all of Klal Yisroel was incomprehensible, let alone his love for the Radiner Rosh Yeshiva. Why then did he only give two minutes of life to R. Naftoli?

When they returned to the yeshiva and told the *olam* what he pledged, a silence shook the room. What? Only two minutes? How could it be? After a few minutes of dismay, one of the *talmidim* stood up and explained the great Chafetz Chaim's pledge. The Chafetz Chaim gave two minutes of his life to R. Naftoli because the Chafetz Chaim knows how precious life is. Two minutes of life to the Chafetz Chaim is 120 seconds of purpose; and that is more precious and priceless than any commodity.

That day made a very big impact on many of those *talmidim* and very possibly changed some of their lives.[268]

In our *parshah*, Bilaam is killed during Klal Yisroel's war with Midian. Many years before, Bilaam served as an advisor on Pharoah's advisory board together with Yisro and Iyov. Bilaam advised Pharaoh to persecute and enslave Klal Yisroel while Iyov remained silent. R. Chaim Shmuelevitz asked: since Iyov's silence was minuscule in comparison to Bilaam's cruel and wicked advice, why wasn't Bilaam's life filled with suffering similar to that of Iyov? All Bilaam suffered was an instant death, while Iyov suffered a life filled with dread, known as "*yisuri Iyov*"!

R. Chaim Shmuelevitz learned from here that the biggest punishment a person can endure is death. Bilaam got his just punishment: the biggest punishment possible, death. Iyov, although he suffered for his silence, he was still alive. We learn from here that even with the greatest of suffering, every single second of life is precious.

Everybody has his or her own "*pekel* of *tzaros*,"[269] Hashem *yerachem*. One of today's challenges is to appreciate life amongst all that suffering. We all want life, and we are all blessed with it. Our hearts pump, our blood continues to flow, and we can walk, talk, and breathe. When we visit acquaintances in a hospital or a grandparent in an old age home, we tend to remind ourselves of how precious life really is. If we could only see what we have and not what we are missing, we might discover that we have the biggest *brachah* around — the gift of life.[270]

---

268 This story is brought in *Meshulchan Govoha*.

269 Bag of pains and misfortunes.

270 Look in the *Chovos Halevavos* at the beginning of *Sha'ar Habechina*.

ONE SHEEP AMONGST SEVENTY WOLVES

PARSHAS MASSEI

וַיִּסְעוּ... וַיַּחֲנוּ (לג, א–מט)
And they journeyed...and they camped.

All forty-two places where Klal Yisroel camped in the Midbar were scorching hot, dry and barren wastelands filled with snakes and scorpions. The only rational explanation of their survival is that Hashem must have taken care of them all those years.[271]

In truth, Hashem is still taking care of us today and our existence is just as miraculous as then.[272] Just think of how many nations have tried to annihilate us over the centuries, and how many have persecuted us with pogroms, libels, and the Holocaust, and yet we still continue to flourish! R. Elchonon Wasserman writes that there were sixteen million socialists in the Socialist Party before World

271 The Rambam says that this is the reason why the Torah was so lengthy in recording all of Klal Yisroel's travels. His explanation can be found in the Ramban at the beginning of our *parshah*.

272 Based on the introduction to the *siddur Bais Yaakov*. It is also brought in *Sifsei Chaim, Moadim*, vol. 3, pg. 253.

War Two. Where are they today? Only Klal Yisroel, the one sheep amongst seventy wolves, is not only surviving but even flourishing. The one possible explanation, says R. Emden, is that Hashem is watching over us and taking care of us, just as He did in the Midbar.[273]

Perhaps this idea can give us comfort in the darkest day of the year, Tishah b'Av. Deep under our sorrow lies Hashem's eternal love and concern for us that shines so brightly. Hiding behind all those pogroms and libels is Hashem's guiding hand. The proof is that we are still around to talk about it. Even after two thousand years, Hashem is still holding on to us and is not letting go.

R. Shimshon Pincus used to tell the story of the time Yankele's father came home dressed in a bear costume and frightened Yankele. Yankele screamed in panic and ran to hide. After his father picked him up and whispered into his ear, "Don't worry Yankele, it's me, Tatty," he was able to tolerate the ferocious bear. All of our pains and anti-Semitism are the bear costume, and the fact that we are still flourishing is Hashem's comforting whisper, "Don't worry, it's Me."

The same is true for the individual as well. Any Jew can draw forth comfort knowing that even in his darkness, Hashem is there, taking care of him.

The *navi* calls Tishah b'Av a *mo'ed*, a holiday.[274] A *mo'ed* is made for rejoicing. This joy stems from that hidden love that is keeping us alive and flourishing even in the darkest of times.

---

273 *Sifsei Chaim, Moadim*, vol. 3, "*Betza'ce me'Mitzrayim…*"

274 That is why we do not say *tachanun* on Tishah b'Av.

SEFER DEVORIM

TO SPEAK, OR NOT TO SPEAK

PARSHAS DEVORIM

אַל תָּצַר אֶת מוֹאָב (ב, ט)
לא אסר להם על מואב אלא מלחמה אבל מיראים היו אותם – רש"י
You shall not distress Moab.

The Chozeh of Lublin had planned to be at a very important meeting in Leipzig. He asked his wife to prepare his bag the night before so that he could catch the first train out in the morning. However, when he returned from *Shacharis*, he discovered that she forgot to prepare his bag. "I thought that I needed to make a *kiddush Hashem* in Leipzig today," he said to himself, "but I see that Hashem wants me to make a *kiddush Hashem* right here." He reacted with silence. He never went to Leipzig and never mentioned anything to his wife.

Together with the *shalom bayis* and peace of mind that emanated from his silence was the eternal reward. The Vilna Gaon writes that for every single second that a person muzzles his mouth (when wanting to say the wrong words), he merits a hidden light of such greatness that no angel or creature can even fathom.[275]

---

275 Look in the *Igeres haGra*.

Not only does silence at the appropriate time bring eternal reward, but choosing the right words when speaking can also create colossal ramifications.

Klal Yisroel was permitted to frighten and provoke the nation of Moav during their travels in the Midbar, but not the nation of Ammon. These guidelines stemmed from an event that happened hundreds of years prior.

Lot had two daughters who lived with him incestuously. Both of them bore sons from that episode. The older daughter shamelessly named her child Moav, which literally means "from father," implying his disgraceful origin. The younger daughter, however, modestly named her son Ben-Ami, "the son of my people" (which was shortened to Ammon), making no direct reference to her father.

Due to the fact that the younger daughter chose a name that did not shame her father, her descendants, Ammon, were spared harassment hundreds of years later. However, the older daughter's descendants, Moav, did not have this merit thanks to the disgraceful name she chose. Consequently, Klal Yisroel was able to frighten them later on in life.[276]

To know whether one should speak, how to speak, or not to speak at all, is a difficult thing to determine, especially under pressure. Perhaps a measuring stick could be if one feels a propelling internal drive to speak, almost as if it is bursting out of him, then he should be very cautious of it, as it might be stemming from an impure source.[277] However, if one finds it difficult to speak, almost as if it he must force it out, chances are it is coming from a pure source and he should then express his thoughts.[278]

---

276 Based on Rashi.

277 In particular his ego. This idea is found in the Vilna Gaon's commentary on *Rus* 1:18. Although it might seem very appropriate at the time, once one's ego calms down, chances are the situation will look very different.

278 Chances are that his ego is not letting him speak. For example, many people find it hard to say thank you, ask for help, or even tell a clerk behind the counter that he received the wrong change. There was once a *bochur* in yeshiva who could not handle his roommate's mess. It got to the point that they were not on speaking terms. Although it might have been hard to communicate his feelings, if he would have just communicated them, he might have saved a broken friendship.

Although it takes work, it is still within our grasp to speak properly and even to be silent at the appropriate times. Perhaps if we remind ourselves of the colossal ramifications, we can accomplish this task that much easier.[279]

279 In particular, now, during the Three Weeks, it is a fitting time to work on our speech, considering that the Beis Hamikdash was destroyed because of our *lashon hara* — the ill use of speech.

A HEALTHY BURDEN

PARSHAS DEVORIM

אֵיכָה אֶשָּׂא לְבַדִּי, טָרְחֲכֶם וּמַשַּׂאֲכֶם וְרִיבְכֶם (א, יב)

How can I carry alone your trouble and your burden and your quarrel?

Mr. Schwartz rushed to the Chafetz Chaim as soon as he noticed a sudden decline in his health. The Chafetz Chaim advised him to go to a certain rav for a *brachah*. Mr. Schwartz went to the rav, received his *brachah*, and soon recovered. Respecting the Chafetz Chaim's wishes to keep his advice a secret, he never told anybody about what happened.

About forty years later, Mr. Schwartz's sister-in-law began to suffer from a similar illness. He revealed the secret and to his sorrow, his illness returned. He rushed back to the Chafetz Chaim to find out what to do. The Chafetz Chaim told him that he was not able to help anymore. "When you came to me long ago, I had enough strength to fast for forty days for your well-being; today I am too old to do that."

Although the Chafetz Chaim only met Mr. Schwartz once, he was still willing to fast forty days on his behalf. This great man was able to feel another Jew's pain as if it was his own.

The Chazon Ish once complained that many people tell him about their pains and sufferings, but very few return to tell him what actually happened. He would end with a sigh, saying that "if only they knew that their problems were my problems, they would surely come back to tell me what happened."[280]

During the last few weeks of Moshe Rabbeinu's life, he hinted to Klal Yisroel some of the things that he had done for them over the years. He told them how hard he "toiled" (טרחכם) to teach them the entire Torah, in spite of the fact that they were a nation that had come from the influences of Mitzrayim. Moshe also told them that he had "carried their burdens" (משאכם), and was very much involved behind the scenes when it came to settling their disputes (ריבכם).[281]

The Ramban understands the phrase "carried your burdens" as a reference to all the *tefillos* that Moshe *davened* for Klal Yisroel.[282] Why did Moshe consider his *tefillos* for Klal Yisroel like burdens?

R. Simcha Ziskind Brody, the late Rosh Yeshiva of Yeshivas Chevron, explains that for a person to classify *davening* for Klal Yisroel as a burden is not a shortcoming, but, on the contrary, it is a great asset.[283]

Many people associate themselves as an outsider when it comes to their friend's trials and tribulations. As a result, they *daven* for their friends and then continue on with their merry lives. However, Moshe Rabbeinu saw another Jew's pains and problems as if it was his own. He could not just daven and then "move on." He felt and carried every Jew's pain in his heart until they were reconciled, the same way he carried his own. If somebody came to Moshe with a broken heart, by the time the conversation ended, Moshe's heart was broken too.

280 This is brought in *Sifsei Chaim, Midos v'Avodas Hashem*, vol. 1, "*Noseh b'ol*" vaad 3.

281 According to Rashi, Moshe Rabbeinu was pointing out to Klal Yisroel their weakness. He told them that they were people who caused trouble (particularly in the *beis din*), spoke critically against their leaders (especially Moshe Rabbeinu) and were ill-tempered. However, the Ramban understands that Moshe was not passing judgment on Klal Yisroel at all for their inadequacies, but rather reminding them of the good that he had done to them over the years.

282 On this *pasuk*.

283 Based on the *Saam Derech*.

Moshe Rabbeinu was telling Klal Yisroel that lying upon his heart were all their burdens, pains, and hardships. He literally "carried their burdens" and consequently *davened* for every Jew with all his might.

In light of this, all of Klal Yisroel's pain and suffering that came from their complaining, quarreling, and even rebelling in the Midbar, were felt by Moshe too.

Moshe Rabbeinu's and the Chafetz Chaim's *tefillos* were a result of their feeling somebody else's pain. Indeed, to feel another person's pain is a lifelong goal. One has to first see past himself and then see the life of others. Perhaps by *davening* for our friends and loved ones with all of our hearts, we can utilize our *tefillos* as a stepping-stone to aid us in our quest. It will allow other people's pains to find a place in our heart, and possibly make us that much better.

PROFESSORS HAVE STUDENTS, ROSHEI YESHIVA HAVE CHILDREN

PARSHAS VA'ESCHANAN

וְשִׁנַּנְתָּם לְבָנֶיךָ (ו, ז) — אלו התלמידים[284]

And teach them (the words of Torah) to your children.

Late one night, at about two in the morning, R. Yaakov Eliezer Schwartzman, Rosh Yeshiva of Lakewood Yerushalayim, was told that one of his *talmidim* was sick in bed. He immediately went to the *talmid*'s apartment to see how he could help. The Rosh Yeshiva made him some tea and pampered him. It must have been about four in the morning when the fever finally broke. The Rosh Yeshiva was filled with so much joy that he started to dance and sing. [The *talmid*'s apartment was adjacent to R. Yitzchok Ezrachi's apartment, one of the Roshei Yeshiva of Yeshivas Mir]. His excitement must have been heard by the neighbors because after a few minutes of dancing and singing, R. Yitzchok Ezrachi walked into the apartment to join in the *simcha*!

What a sight to see, two giant Roshei Yeshiva, dancing around the

284 *Sifrei*, brought in Rashi.

bed of a *talmid* at four o'clock in the morning. Now, can you picture a college professor visiting his sick student in bed and dancing for joy when his student's fever broke? Obviously not! The difference is clear: professors have students and Roshei Yeshiva have children.

The Sifrei explains that the word *le'vanecha* — your children,[285] also refers to *talmidim*. The reason why the Torah included *talmidim* in the word "children," and did not write it separately,[286] was to hint to us that our *talmidim* are our children too.

R. Aharon Kotler loved every single *talmid* in the yeshiva as his own child. Once, in the middle of the Simchas Torah *hakafos*, amongst all the singing and dancing, R. Aharon whispered into a *talmid*'s ear and the *talmid* immediately stopped singing. Later, his friends asked him, "What did the Rosh Yeshiva tell you?" He shyly answered, "He reminded me that I have a *shidduch motzaei Yom Tov*, and should be careful not to strain my voice during the dancing."

Only a father or a *rebbi* (who is likened to a father) thinks such thoughts in the heat of the Simchas Torah dancing. This was R. Aharon.

Teachers and *rebbeim* alike must know that their *talmidim* are not only their *talmidim;* they are also their children. R. Yechezkol Sarna writes that only with such love and concern can one truly make *talmidim*.[287]

285 "And teach them [the words of the Torah] to your children."

286 "Teach them to your children and your *talmidim*."

287 Brought in *Mi'shulchan Govoah*.

SEEING HOW HASHEM "DELIVERS THE GOODS"

BIRCAS HA-MAZON

PARSHAS EIKEV

וְאָכַלְתָּ וְשָׂבָעְתָּ וּבֵרַכְתָּ אֶת ה' אֱלֹקֶיךָ (ח, י)

You will eat and you will be satisfied, and bless Hashem.

The mitzvah of *bircas hamazon* has an interesting origin. It was formulated over the course of Klal Yisroel's history. Moshe Rabbeinu in the wilderness ordained the first paragraph of *Hazan Es Haolam* when the *mann* started to fall from heaven. Yehoshua ben Nun added *Nodeh Lecha* when Klal Yisroel entered Eretz Yisroel, and finally Dovid haMelech and Shlomo haMelech added *Rachem* and *Uvenei Yerushalayim* when they merited building Yerushalayim and the Beis Hamikdash.[288]

However, we all know that adding or subtracting from the Torah's commandments is strictly forbidden.[289] If so, why weren't these additions prohibited by Torah law?[290]

---

288 Look in *Brachos* 48b.

289 This prohibition is found in last week's *parshah*, *Va'eschanan*.

290 Based on a *shmooze* that R. Yisroel Newman *shlita*, one of the Roshei Yeshiva

By reflecting on the *nusach* of the *bircas hamazon* that Moshe, Yehoshua, Dovid, and Shlomo established, we can actually answer our question. We see that the mitzvah of *bircas hamazon* is not just to thank Hashem for the food that He gives us, but to notice also how He delivers it as well. To become aware of that "pipeline" is part of the mitzvah too.

With this, we can understand why the additions to *bircas hamazon* are in line with what the Torah sanctions, since the mitzvah is not only to thank Hashem, but also to see how Hashem bestows His kindness upon us.

When we were in the wilderness, Hashem gave us our needs directly from Heaven, therefore Moshe formulated the *bircas hamazon* accordingly, referring to *mann* from Heaven. So too, when we entered Eretz Yisroel, the "pipeline" that brought Hashem's kindness into the world was Eretz Yisroel, and finally through the Beis Hamikdash, which explains Dovid and Shlomo's addition.

Being aware of the good that Hashem gives and appreciating how He gives it to us is a valuable lesson that can enhance our sense of gratitude towards Him and make our *avodas Hashem* that much stronger.

In truth, this can be applied to all of our *brachos*. Just look at how Hashem brings a person a cup of coffee.[291] Coffee beans are grown mainly in Brazil. Someone plants the trees and takes care of them until the coffee beans reach maturity. Then workers pick the beans from the trees. The beans are then roasted, ground, and packed for shipping. Then there is all the work involved within the packaging and shipping industries, which allows the coffee beans to reach their destination. This alone requires hundreds of people.

Finally, the coffee arrives at the port from where it is taken to grocery stores for sales. Within the house, we have a gas range that boils the water, the kettle that whistles, and the matches that light the flame (before matches, people rubbed two sticks together). Then

---

of Beis Medrash Govoha, Lakewood, New Jersey, said in Lakewood Yerushalayim's first Elul in Ramot 5764.

291 Based on R. Zelig Pliskin, *Gateway to Happiness*, pg. 34.

there is the milk and sugar, which adds flavor and color to the coffee. Tens, if not hundreds of people work to bring your cup of coffee to you so you can enjoy it. This is all without mentioning the cup, saucer, teaspoon, and table to place it on, and the chair to sit on while drinking it.

If we think for a moment before we recite *bircas hamazon*, or any *brachah* for that matter, how Hashem "delivers the goods," we can build inside of ourselves a deeper love and appreciation of what He does for us.

IT IS GOOD TO BE CHASED EVERY ONCE IN A WHILE

PARSHAS RE'EH

לֹא תְאַמֵּץ אֶת לְבָבְךָ... כִּי פָתֹחַ תִּפְתַּח אֶת יָדְךָ (טו, א–יא)
You should not harden your heart... Rather you should open your hand to him.

A man once came to the home where the Chafetz Chaim was a guest. He was seeking council on a pressing issue that was bothering him and his family. The host invited him into the room where the Chafetz Chaim was eating lunch and the man sat down near the Chafetz Chaim and waited patiently for him to finish.

The Chafetz Chaim was accustomed to sing *Mizmor le'Dovid* at the end of his meal prior to *bircas hamazon.* When he reached the last *pasuk, "Ach tov v'chessed yirdefooni kol yemei chayai* — Only goodness and kindness should chase after me all the days of my life," he turned to the honorable visitor, whom he had never seen before, and asked him in sheer bewilderment, "How can Dovid haMelech ask that only goodness and kindness should chase after him all the days of his life? 'Chase' is a derogatory term used to describe a pursuer or hunter. Surely, goodness and kindness are not chasers and hunters. And why does he ask that they should chase him all the days of his life?"

The Chafetz Chaim answered his own question. "Sometimes it appears to a person that his involvement in doing acts of kindness and goodness are chasing after him, stealing his time, and tormenting him and his family. He begins to think that his participation in this act of kindness is destroying his business and causing other matters to suffer. His *yetzer hara* convinces him to refrain from doing those kind acts in order not to lose out. He eventually views these acts of kindness as pursuers that are jeopardizing his life.

"Dovid haMelech was teaching us that even if the acts of kindness that we perform appear as if they are chasing us and threatening us, nonetheless we should not forsake them at all. Instead, we should ask that they pursue us continually all the days of our lives."

The Chafetz Chaim concluded, "Not only will they save us from harm and misfortune, they will also bring us eternal happiness and beauty."

As soon as the Chafetz Chaim finished, the guest got up from his seat and headed towards the door. The host was puzzled. "You didn't even ask the Chafetz Chaim's advice and you are leaving?" The guest replied, "I already received my answer before I had a chance to ask my question!"

The guest explained to the host that a few years ago he had established two *gemachim*. Those *gemachim* were now "stealing" his time to the point that his wife said, "Enough is enough. You must give the management of these *gemachim* over to somebody else in the community so that you can have your life back." However, that did not seem right to him. Therefore, he and his wife came up with a solution: to seek the guidance of the great Chafetz Chaim. When he heard the Chafetz Chaim say that even when the kindness seems like a hunter chasing after you you must continue doing the acts of kindness because they will bring you eternity, he received his answer before he had a chance to ask his question.

There is nothing more precious than a mitzvah, a word of Torah, or an opportunity to help another Jew. These things illuminate our world and build our eternity. Sometimes we are tricked to believe that the most precious things in life are actually "chasers" or things that are jeopardizing our lives, when in truth they are there to make our lives that much better.

HELPING OTHERS BELIEVE IN THEMSELVES

PARSHAS SHOFTIM

יָדֵינוּ לֹא שָׁפְכוּ אֶת הַדָּם הַזֶּה (כא, ז)
Our hands have not spilled this blood.

If a dead body is found in a field between two cities without any knowledge of who murdered him, the elders of the city closest to the corpse must perform the mitzvah of *Eglah Arufah* (the axed heifer). They begin the mitzvah by declaring that they were not responsible for the murder. "The elders shall speak up and say, 'Our hands have not spilled this blood and our eyes have not witnessed it.'"

The implication of their declaration is that they were suspected of murder. This is difficult to understand, since the elders were the elite of the city, not only judicially, but also in their piety. How can the Torah insinuate that they were the perpetrators of the murder?

Rashi writes that the elders who make this statement were attesting to the fact that they never met the victim or had any part in his leaving the city without food and without an escort.

However, this too needs an explanation. Their declaration is not that they never met him, but rather that they "did not spill his blood." How does Rashi's explanation fit with their declaration? Moreover, even if they were guilty of not escorting him with the proper provisions for the way, does that allow the Torah to call them murderers? Surely not. If so, why does the Torah attribute to them such a dramatic title?

R. Simcha Zissel, the Alter of Kelm, gives an amazing answer.[292] A person who departs from a city unescorted may begin to feel about himself that he is unloved and unappreciated. These insecurities may eliminate the lack the confidence needed to ward off bandits and ambushers along the way if he is attacked.

However, if the elders of the city knew the deceased and escorted him, they would have provided him with the emotional support needed to stand up against any bandits along the way. However, if they knew him and did not escort him, they could have been the cause of his insecurities and as such would be held accountable for his death — to the degree that the Torah would have called them murderers. With this, we can see how Rashi's explanation fits into the *pasuk*, because by not escorting him, they were in essence leading him to his deadly fate.

When we show people that we are concerned and care for their well-being, we are actually granting them an inner strength to believe in themselves. If the elders would have known the deceased and given him the support he needed, he would have believed in himself to the point that he would have fought for his life against the murderer.

The great *Tanna* Rabbi Akiva is a prime example of how believing in somebody can make all the difference. When he was forty years old, he was just a mere shepherd who did not even know the *alef beis*, and yet after his wife believed in him, he blossomed into becoming the great Rabbi Akiva with twenty-four thousand *talmidim*.

When we show people that we believe in them and care for them, we are actually unearthing their potential storehouses of energy and strength. When a *rebbi* believes in his *talmid*, the *talmid* shines with

---

292 Look in *Darchei Mussar*.

inner self-confidence: "I can do it, my *rebbi* believes in me!" So too a child can shine with that beautiful inner self-confidence when his parents believe in him.

If the elders of the city would have known the deceased and would have shown him the care and concern he needed, he would have somehow survived the murder, and if they did not, they then would have been held accountable for "spilling his blood." From here we see when we care and believe in somebody, they care and believe in themselves.

A House, a Vineyard, and an Ox

Parshas Ki Seitzei

כִּי יִקָּרֵא קַן צִפּוֹר... כִּי תִבְנֶה בַּיִת חָדָשׁ (כב, ו–יד)

If a bird's nest happens before you...If you build a new house...

Chazal teach us that the performance of one mitzvah, even a minor one, creates a spiritual chain reaction that opens up opportunities for other mitzvos to follow, no matter what the cost. Chazal call this natural phenomenon *"mitzvah goreres mitzvah"* — that one mitzvah brings another mitzvah. With this concept, Rashi explains how seven seemingly unrelated *pesukim* are, in truth, related.

The first two of the seven *pesukim* discuss the mitzvah of *shiluach hakein* — sending away the mother bird from her nest. Rashi explains that one who performs this mitzvah will merit another mitzvah: the mitzvah of *ma'akah* — putting a fence around one's roof.[293] Since it is impossible to perform the mitzvah of *ma'akah* without a home, Hashem will grant him a home to facilitate it. Hence, the mitzvah of *shiluach ha-kein* brought about the mitzvah of *ma'akah*, which actually caused him to have a home.

293 *Pasuk* 8.

After he fences his roof, Hashem will give him the opportunity to fulfill the mitzvah of *kilayim*,[294] which is the fourth *pasuk* in our list of seven.[295] Since one cannot fulfill this mitzvah without a vineyard, Hashem will grant him a vineyard. Then, Hashem will grant him a field, oxen, and donkeys in order to fulfill the negative mitzvah of not plowing with a donkey and ox simultaneously,[296] and so on and so forth.

This spiritual chain reaction is so significant that Hashem will provide him with whatever he needs in order to facilitate the next mitzvah — be it a house, vineyard, field, or donkeys and oxen for that matter.

The Be'er Yosef understands that if a person who executed the mitzvah of *shiluach ha-kein* would not put a fence on the roof of his home, he would be causing himself to lose his home! He did not receive his home as a reward for performing the preceding mitzvah; it was given to him in order to fulfill the next mitzvah of *ma'akah*. Therefore, if he does not place a fence on it, he would be forgoing his rights to the home.[297]

Rashi brings *Targum Onkelos* that translates the word *ma'akah* (fence) in the *pasuk* as *takia*, which means "a bag." Rashi explains that the fence around the rooftop protects the people that are inside of it from falling, just as a bag protects what is inside of it.

However, the Be'er Yosef explains that the fence protects the house itself for its owners. It enables them to hold onto it. Since the whole reason why he merited this house was in order to fulfill the mitzvah associated with it, when he fulfills that mitzvah, he is in truth insuring the security of his home, just as a bag insures the security of its contents.

Within this Rashi lies an eye-opening insight into all of our acquisitions. We should not amass acquisitions for the sake of owning them. Rather, we should view our acquisitions in light of

294 This is the negative mitzvah of not planting different species in a vineyard.

295 *Pasuk* 9.

296 *Pasuk* 10.

297 R. Yosef from Salant.

the mitzvahs that we can do with them. It could be that the sole reason why somebody has a specific possession is in order to do a certain mitzvah with it. It follows from this that life is about amassing mitzvahs, not acquisitions; the acquisitions are secondary to the mitzvah. They are there to help us in our performance of the mitzvah.

Happiness Is Dependent on Our Attitude, Not Our Situation

Parshas Ki Savo

וְשָׂמַחְתָּ בְכָל הַטּוֹב (כו, יא)

And you shall rejoice with all the goodness that Hashem... has given you.

The *bikkurim* ceremony during the times of the Beis Hamikdash was something quite extraordinary. The Mishnah describes how the farmers brought their *bikkurim* in decorative baskets, overflowing with luscious fruits.[298] Farmers from all over Eretz Yisroel filled the streets. Everybody was eager to bring up their first fruits as an expression of gratitude to Hashem for His bountiful kindness. There were flutes and bands playing music, and horns of oxen were ornamented with golden embroidery to make it such a joyous and auspicious occasion. They were days of sheer happiness and delight.

298 *Bikkurim*, perek 3.

Why then, asks R. Mordechai Gifter, does the Torah have to command the people who brought their *bikkurim* to be happy and rejoice? Why wasn't rejoicing a natural outcome of the situation itself?[299]

R. Gifter understands from here that even the most perfect situation, like the *bikkurim* ceremony, cannot guarantee happiness. Despite all the potential joy that accompanied the ceremony, the Torah still had to command the person bringing his *bikkurim* to be happy and rejoice.

The *Chovos Halevavos* gives us the insight into understanding why.[300] He explains that since man has an inclination to always want more, he does not appreciate what he already has.[301] This inclination can blind a person to the degree that no matter what the situation has to offer, his wanting more causes him to become dissatisfied with what he presently has. Therefore, regardless of the circumstances, no situation can assure happiness, because one is likely to find dissatisfaction in it.

Similarly with the *bikkurim* ceremony, even amongst all the excitement and festivities lies the potential for a disappointed farmer. Despite his overflowing basket, he still might be inclined to think, "Why is his basket prettier than mine? Why is the fruit superior to mine? Oy, I wish my field would have produced better fruits!" This attitude can turn a potentially joyous event into a gloomy experience.

The Torah, by commanding these farmers to be happy, is teaching us that situations do not bring happiness and joy; it is our attitude that brings them. Statements like, "If I only had this, then I would be happy," or "All I need is that, and then everything will be fine," not only steal from a person the happiness that he could have acquired from his present situation, but blinds him from seeing all the other goodness that he now possesses.

The *Chovos Halevavos* tells us that with the proper attitude one

---

299 *Pirkei Torah* on the Torah, vol 2, brought in R. Zelig Pliskin, *Growth Through Torah*.

300 Look in the introduction to *Sha'ar Habichina*.

301 Chazal teach in *Koheles Rabbah*: "He who has one hundred wants two hundred."

can find joy no matter what the situation[302] — be it a burnt cake, a missed phone call, or not finding a parking space. The right attitude can turn any situation into a positive experience. This attitude is found in the Torah's command to the farmers: "You shall rejoice, with all the goodness, that Hashem has given you." One should find his happiness with all the goodness that he already has, and not let the constant yearning for new and improved things blind him.

There are individuals that have it "all" — a wonderful home, a good job, a healthy family and more — yet they still feel they have nothing, while there are people that seemingly have nothing, but they appear as if they have everything. The explanation is that happiness is dependent on one's attitude, not on one's particular situation or circumstance.

One should not wait for the ideal situation to deliver the happiness and joy because it may never come. The potential for happiness is dependent upon us and our attitude.

Let us try and adopt the attitude of appreciating what we have, thus finding the good from within, as opposed to letting the thought of what we could have had or should have had darken our day.

---

302 In his introduction to *Sha'ar Habitachon*.

THE CAKE FLOPPED

PARSHAS NITZAVIM

וּבָחַרְתָּ בַּחַיִּים... (ל, יט)
And you shall choose life...

Mrs. Newman was very excited to bake a cake for her new neighbors. She exerted much effort in finding the right recipe, buying all the necessary ingredients, and finally baking it. However, on her way over to deliver the cake, a cyclist bumped into her from behind and there went the cake.

It is important to know when it comes to doing mitzvos that *bitachon*, relying on Hashem's aid, plays a very significant role. Although there is no place for *bitachon* when it comes to *choosing* to do a mitzvah or in exerting the effort needed to try to implement our choice, nonetheless the actual doing of the mitzvah is not up to us, but to Hashem. He decides if our attempts will be actualized or not, and for that we need *bitachon*.[303]

Mrs. Newman not succeeding in actually delivering the cake was not up to her. For some reason Hashem did not want it to be delivered. In such an event, her job is to have *bitachon* in Hashem and believe that whatever happened was for the best.

---

303 Look in *Chovos Halevavos, Shaar Habitachon*, ch. 4, the fourth and fifth part.

Therefore, to say that Mrs. Newman failed would not be true, because she actually succeeded in doing all the aspects of the mitzvah that were entirely up to her. She chose to do an act of *chessed* and exerted much effort in doing so.[304]

R. Yisroel Salanter summed this up by saying that all we need to do is try, not produce; the production is in Hashem's hands.[305]

The truth is that even though her efforts were not actualized, she will still receive a reward for her choice and efforts invested toward doing the mitzvah. Perhaps we can view Mrs. Newman's challenge in a different light and see yet another aspect of success. If Mrs. Newman's children knew what happened and witnessed her positive reaction, she could have instilled into her children by way of example the correct Torah outlook toward mitzvos, and that happiness does not depend on results.

In conclusion, people should not feel down or upset when their efforts are not actualized, because the actualization is not up to us, but to Hashem. If you chose and tried to do the right thing, know that you have succeeded. Don't let the final product rob you of that success.[306]

---

304 Look in *Derech Hashem* 1:3:12 at the end.

305 Look in the *Sifsei Chaim, Moadim*, vol. 2, pg. 47, in the footnote: "*Man daf ton, an nishet off ton.*"

306 Because if one tries hard enough, Hashem will help that person achieve his goals.

INSTILLING A LOVE FOR MITZVOS

PARSHAS NITZAVIM

וּבָחַרְתָּ בַּחַיִּים, לְמַעַן תִּחְיֶה, אַתָּה וְזַרְעֶךָ (ל, יט)

Choose life, so that you will live, you and your offspring.

As Mr. Rosenberg was pulling out of his driveway with over two hundred *mishloach manos* baskets, his nine-year-old son Moishe came running after him. "Tatty, Tatty," he cried, "I want to come with you!"

Mr. Rosenberg stopped the car and let him in and off they went. Mr. Rosenberg became the official "driver" and Moishe became the designated "delivery boy" of the *mishloach manos*. The hustle and bustle, the running around, the opportunity to put a smile on other people's faces, made an everlasting impression on Moishe.

It may have looked like Mr. Rosenberg was just letting Moishe come along for the ride, but in truth he was instilling in his son a love for mitzvos. Mr. and Mrs. Rosenberg's deep-seated love for mitzvos, and in particular the mitzvah of *mishloach manos*, was so great that it was able to ignite in Moishe a love and appreciation towards mitzvos as well.

Many years later, when Moishe started his own family, he continued the tradition of giving out hundreds of *mishloach manos*. This time, however, Moishe was the official "driver" and his young son, Yossi, was the designated "delivery boy." After Yossi had delivered *mishloach manos* to a few of the less popular boys in his class, he ran back to the car, looked at his father with the biggest smile and said, "Tatty, I feel like I just hit a home run! Doing mitzvos is awesome!"[307]

R. Moshe Feinstein understands that when the Torah writes, "Choose life, so that you will live, you and your offspring," it is not giving us an incentive to do mitzvos, as if the Torah is saying if we choose life then our children will follow. Rather, the Torah is showing us how much love and appreciation parents should personally have for mitzvos.[308] The degree of love should be so great that it should influence and ignite in one's children a desire to "live" as well,[309] like Mr. and Mrs. Rosenberg managed to do. They were so enthusiastic about their *Yiddishkeit* that it became contagious. They loved the Torah and mitzvos with such passion that their children also wanted to perform them with that very passion.

One step beyond the internal love and appreciation found in a parent's heart is the verbal expression of that love. When parents tell their children that they are excited to do a mitzvah and enjoy doing it, it has a stronger impact on their children. For example: "I love calling Bubby and Zeide every day." "I feel so fortunate to have such a beautiful family; I can't wait to *daven* and thank Hashem." "I am so excited for this Shabbos; we invited a new family that just moved into the neighborhood."

Conversely, parents who view the Torah as a heavy burden and keep the mitzvos only because they "have to" are not "choosing life" according to the Torah's standards. They are not expressing a personal love or appreciation for their *Yiddishkeit* in a way that excites their children. Unfortunately, they tend to create an atmosphere of

---

307 Based on a story I saw in Slovie Jungreis-Wolf, *Raising Children with Soul* (New York: St. Martin Griffin).

308 In *Darash Moshe*.

309 In *yeshivish* terms, we would say that למען תחיה אתה וזרעך is a שיעור in the mitzvah of ובחרת בחיים.

reluctance and lack of enthusiasm towards the Torah and its mitzvos.

When it comes to parenting, we must remember that our role as parents is to generate our own personal love and appreciation towards the Torah and its mitzvos, i.e., to "choose life" and cherish it. We know that we have "chosen life" when that love and appreciation overflows onto our children.

BROADENING OUT

PARSHAS VAYELECH

ה' אֱלֹהֶיךָ הוּא עֹבֵר לְפָנֶיךָ (לא, ג)
Hashem, your G-d, He will cross before you.

A *bochur* had asked R. Shach to look into a certain *shidduch* two days before R. Shach's *rebbitzen* was *nifteres*. On the way home from the *levayah*, R. Shach spotted the *bochur* and gestured that he come over. He told him that he had checked out the *shidduch* and thought that it was a good idea.

If we could look into R. Shach's heart, we would most probably find a heart broad enough to handle all of Klal Yisroel's problems, as we see that even at his wife's *levayah* he was concerned about that *bochur*'s needs.

The Chafetz Chaim's heart also stretched to fit in all of Klal Yisroel. He spent twenty-five years of his life writing the *Mishnah Berurah* to help those who couldn't decipher halachah properly.[310] He also

310 He also believed that every Jew had the capability to finish the Rif's (Rav Alfasi) commentary on *Shas*. (He understood that *Shas* seemed too big for many people to finish, and since the *Rif* is basically a synopsis of the Gemara according to halachah, and much smaller, he understood that it was most definitely in everybody's grasp.) The only problem was that the Rif did not comment on every *mesechta*. So the Chafetz Chaim wrote a "Rif" on the *masechtos* that did not already have the Rif's commentary. He based it on the Rambam, *Kesef*

wrote a guidebook for Jewish soldiers who found it difficult to keep halachah in the army; the book told them where they could be lenient in times of need. He was afraid that *lashon hara* would destroy us so he wrote the world renowned *Chafetz Chaim*, which compiles all the laws of *lashon hara*. He also wrote countless books filled with stories, parables, and *chizuk* to aid us in our quest for truth.

The Chafetz Chaim's concerns were to alleviate our pain and suffering as well as to help us serve Hashem better. Perhaps we can say that he gave his entire self over for the betterment of Klal Yisoel.

Such an attribute seems to be part of the basic criteria for a true leader of Klal Yisroel. Moshe Rabbeinu was about to pass away and he was concerned about Klal Yisroel's worries. "Perhaps they are worried that after I will pass away they will not have a leader anymore." He told them not to worry because they were going to have an even better leader.

Moshe was about to die and all of his concerns were for Klal Yisroel's fears? Yes, because that is a real leader.

We are not born being leaders; we must begin by broadening our concerns. If we are also concerned about what our family wants, then we can spread out to the concerns of our community, and from there to all of Klal Yisroel.

Mishna, and other earlier commentaries and called it "*Lekutei Halachos*." Look in *Lekutei Amorim* by the Chafetz Chaim, ch. 9.

THE ULTIMATE JUSTICE

PARSHAS HA'AZINU

קֵ-ל אֱמוּנָה, וְאֵין עָוֶל (לב, ד)
A G-d of faith, never unjust.

Is the attribute "never unjust" an honorable or respectable way to praise Hashem? Hashem's ways are perfect, and His attributes are compassion and mercy. "Never unjust" is a term that seems to be very beneath Him. What deep secret is hiding behind this praise?

The answer is that the Torah works with Godly definitions, not human ones.[311] Therefore, when the Torah tells us that Hashem is never unjust or unfair, it is referring to something very colossal. It is teaching us that Hashem's justice extends far beyond the one who He directly punished. His justice reaches to every nook and cranny of every ramification and consequence possible. Let us give an example:

When a judge tries a criminal and sentences him to a lifetime in prison, even if we assume that his punishment fits his crime, what about his family? Why do they have to suffer? What did they do

311 Brought in the *Me'am Loez* in the name of the Yosef Lekach. The essay was taken from *Otzeros Hatorah*, courtesy of the author, HaRav Eliyahu Chaim Cohen *shlita*.

wrong? Aside from ruining their name, the criminal's wife will be left alone without a husband and breadwinner and his children will be left fatherless. Where is the justice in that? The answer is that there is no justice. Human judgment, disappointingly so, has its limitations. It has to proceed with a sentence even when the consequences will be unjust and unfair.

However, Hashem's rulings are very different. Every single punishment that every person will ever receive is planned out, organized, and catered precisely to fit the amount that the criminal, or anyone affected by it, deserves. There is no injustice in anything that Hashem does.

This is beyond our human comprehension and is absolutely mind-boggling. Our world, with all of its inhabitants, is a very interwoven and entwined network. Reuven knows Shimon, and Shimon knows Levi, etc. This attribute of "never unjust" is teaching us that Hashem will not punish Reuven in a way that will pain Shimon if Shimon does not deserve that pain.

The many calculations that have to be made before Hashem can punish somebody are endless and awe-inspiring. The world is a very complicated jigsaw puzzle that only Hashem knows how to put together. "Never unjust" touches that magic and praises Hashem for it. Hashem is "never unjust." Hashem precisely measures every single ounce of pain and suffering that every single person will ever have to bear. Now that is awesome.

This is why R. Eliyahu Lopian would advise people to make themselves "needed" by individuals and the community. He would say that it could potentially save them from an evil decree. He would explain that even if the person did something wrong and was deserving of punishment, nonetheless if the ramifications of his punishment would reach others who did not deserve to suffer at all, Hashem would not punish him.

Based on this idea as well, the Chazon Ish would advise people against life insurance. He would explain that there are people in the world that do not deserve to live. However, Hashem lets them live because they support their wives and children. If such a person would have life insurance, he would lose his merit to live. Once his family would not need him to be "the breadwinner" of the home because of the life insurance, Hashem could take him away.[312]

Hashem's ways are nothing less than awesome. Just to contemplate for a moment our interwoven world and all the ramifications that can transpire after every ruling, and then knowing that there is no injustice is nothing less than mindboggling. Let's always remember, in any situation we find ourselves, that Hashem, the One who provides us with everything, is never unjust.

---

312 I heard that R. Volbe and many others were in favor of life insurance.

REJOICING OVER YOUR FRIEND'S FORTUNE

PARSHAS V'ZOS HABRACHAH

וַיַּרְאֵהוּ ה' אֶת כָּל הָאָרֶץ (לד, א)

And Hashem showed him the entire land.

Aside from teaching her students the beauty of *Yiddishkeit*, Mrs. Zelda Rosenthal taught her students how to rejoice when their friends succeeded.

After they finished playing their first game of the semester, she turned to the losing team and asked them, "Who is happy for the winning team?" Only one child raised her hand. She rewarded her and the winning team with a small prize. Already by the second game the children had caught on and when she asked the losers the same question, they all raised their hands. This time, she rewarded everybody.[313]

She would teach the children that it is important to do your best, enjoy the game, and most of all to be happy for the winner.

Even though Moshe Rabbeinu was not personally allowed to enter into Eretz Yisroel, nonetheless Hashem still wanted to show him its

---

313 Zelda B. Rosenthal, *Precious Jewels* (Artscroll), pg. 216.

beauty. Hashem knew that Moshe would rejoice in seeing the beautiful gift that the nation he loved so dearly would receive.

Moshe's own deep-seated passion to enter the land did not stop his heart from singing with joy as he saw the lavish and wonderful land that Klal Yisroel would receive. He was beyond any form of jealousy.

Both Esti and Dini were planning for their end-of-the-year field trips. Esti's was on Sunday and Dini's was on Tuesday. Sunday morning came and to her disappointment, Esti woke up with a fever of 101 degrees and was not able to go. She called her sister Dini into the room and said, "Dini, I already packed my bag with all my favorite candies. I am not going on my field trip because I am sick. If you want, you can take my candies for your trip on Tuesday. I am sure you would love them; they are really yummy and are my favorite."

Nothing is more beautiful than watching a selfless heart in action.

MOADIM

MOADIM U'ZMANIM

ARE YOU EXPERIENCED?

We all go through experiences, but not all of us grow from them. For many people experiences end as a memory. However, experiences could be much more than a memory; they could enrich our lives, our *hashkafos*, and even ourselves.

"Don't let your experiences just be a memory," R. Hutner would say to his *talmidim*. "Take your experiences along with you and become a better person."

The secret is to allow our experiences to touch our hearts and to teach us how to become better people.

The thousands of seminary girls and yeshiva *bochurim* who have come to Eretz Yisroel over the decades to study can be an example to help us understand what R. Hutner meant. Many of them come to Eretz Yisroel and find themselves walking away with an SD card filled with countless pictures and various memories. If they would utilize their experiences to learn how to live their lives, they would also walk away being better people.

Take, for example, a seminary girl who was a *bas bayis* by a family for the year. If she learned how to run a home and become a good mother, then her experience was not just an experience

— it transformed her into a better and more beautiful person. Consequently, her experience became part of her essence.

Bochurim could utilize their years in yeshiva to mold their *haskafos* and shape themselves into true *bnei Torah*. Consequently, their yeshiva year in Eretz Yisroel would not only end as a memory, but would become a part of their inner being.

Allowing our experiences to become our teachers can also help us transform all the *Moadim* into a time of self-growth. Take the month of Tishrei; instead of just "experiencing" Rosh Hashanah, *Aseres Yemei Teshuvah*, Yom Kippur, and Succos, we can actually utilize these days to enrich our *hashkafos* and ourselves.

Chazal have taught us that there are at least four major lessons to be taken out of the month of Tishrei: that Hashem is King of the Universe, a Helper, a Savior, and a Shield for us. Just as He was coronated King on Rosh Hashanah, helped us do *teshuvah* during the *Aseres Yemei Teshuvah*, saved us from the consequences of our sins on Yom Kippur, and protected us on Succos, so too He will do that for us for the rest of the year and for all time.

Chazal felt that such knowledge is so vital to us that they incorporated these lessons into our *Shemoneh Esrei. Melech, Ozer, U'Moshia, U'Magen (King, Helper, Savior and Shield)* is there to remind us of the lessons we have gathered from the month of Tishrei.[314]

If we are willing to make our experiences our teachers, they will be much more than a memory — they will become part of us. Don't just walk away from the month of Tishrei, or any *mo'ed* for that matter, with a memory; take something with you![315]

---

314 Based on the *Siddur Sha'arei Shamayim's* explanation of *Melech, Ozer...*

315 Look in *Sha'arei Teshuva*, 2:1. *"Yal'deh yom ya'ku'shoon machshavusecha..."*

ELUL

THE JEWISH CALENDAR

It was *erev* Succos and Yankele's father was going to Geulah to buy his *lulav*. Now, Geulah on *erev chag* is not the best place to take a nine-year-old boy. The floods of people, combined with the pressure of finding a nice *lulav*, could cause such a boy to be washed away, never to be seen again. Little Yankele, however, was very eager to tag along, and knew that with enough persistence his father would take him. Soon they boarded the bus together, heading for Geulah.[316]

It wasn't long before Yankele's father dove into a box of *lulavim* and started his hunt. "Now, Yankele, hold on to my jacket very tightly and don't let go," he told his soon. "I'm going to look in this box for a *lulav*, and with the *Eibishter's* help, we'll find one soon enough!"

Fifteen minutes later, Yankele's father lifted his head and said, "*Baruch Hashem*! Yankele, I found the perfect *lu...lav*... Yankele... Yankele...where are you? Where is my Yankele?" Yankele had disappeared!

Meanwhile, Yankele felt as if he had just escaped from the zoo. He was having the time of his life, taking candies from the candy

316 Based on a talk I once heard from R. Shimshon Pincus, *zt"l*.

store and throwing sticks and stones at all sorts of things. He even managed to break a window or two. Suddenly, someone grabbed him by the arm and said, "Hey, kid, where's your father?" Yankele's excitement immediately changed to piercing cries of panic as his body shook with fear.

The stranger took Yankele to the lost-and-found section of the police station, where he sat sniffling, waiting for his father to come and find him. Between sniffles, he cried to himself, *Why did I let go of my Tatty?*

Yankele's father was beside himself. He ran around frantically, searching for his son, until finally somebody suggested that he try the police station.

When he walked in, the officer inquired, "How can l help you, sir?"

"Is my son here?" Yankele's father replied.

The officer said, "Sir, to claim a child, you need proof that he is yours. And if there are charges against him, are you prepared to pay the charges?"

Just then, Yankele looked up and saw his father. Without a moment's delay, he leaped into his arms and cried, "Taaatttyyy!! I'm sorry, Tatty. I'm sorry I left you. I'll never leave you again."

As Tatty's heart melted from the hug, he forgot all about his frantic search. With Yankele in his arms, he turned to the door, ready to leave the station.

The officer stopped him. "Sir, what about the charges?"

Tatty handed over a sum of money to cover the claims, and he and Yankele happily went home.

The story does not end there. Yankele had missed his father so much that he decided to sleep with him that night, and for days after, tag along with him wherever he went, always regretting that day in Geulah when he had let go of his father.

Yankele is a *mashal* for Klal Yisroel.

The Jewish year begins with us holding onto Hashem's hand during those holy days of *deveikus:* Rosh Hashanah, Yom Kippur, Succos, and Simchas Torah. However, throughout the course of the year, we tend to loosen our grip, getting a bit too caught up in the physical world, and begin to wander away from Hashem, just as Yankele did when he and his father arrived in Geulah. We find ourselves doing things that we should not be doing and enjoying ourselves without reflecting on the ramifications of our actions. This is similar to Yankele's gallivanting around Geulah, stealing candies and throwing stones.

When the year comes to a close with the months of Av and Elul, we begin to wake up and realize how far we have wandered and how deadly our sins really are. The month of Av, with all of its calamities, reminds us that letting go of Hashem's hand is not as glamorous as it once appeared. The breaking of the *luchos* and the destruction of the Beis Hamikdash occurred because we "let go" of Hashem's hand.

The month of Av, however, also helps us awaken feelings of remorse, reminding us that we wish we had never gotten so caught up with the physical world the way we did. These feelings help a Jew walk into Elul already wanting to change for the better.

Yankele's cries of fear, while waiting for his father in the police station, are like the daily shofar blasts of the month of Elul. Just as he wondered, *Am I going to get in trouble for the wrongs I did? How will I pay for all that damage? Will my father still love me and accept me back with open arms?* — so too, we regret the past and wonder what the future will look like.

Finally, that heart-melting cry, "*Tatty!*" as Yankele leaped into his father's arms, is like the blast of the shofar on Rosh Hashanah. That moment is probably the most precious and stirring moment of the whole year. At its deepest level, the loud shofar blast is when we whisper into Hashem's ear, "I'm sorry I left you, I will never leave you again." That shofar blast takes us to the *Kodesh haKodashim*, where we can, *kaveyachol*, touch Hashem's heart and create a completely new relationship for the upcoming year and the rest of our lives.

With this leap into Hashem's arms and our promise that we will never leave Him again, we awaken Hashem's will, *kaveyachol*, to pay for the "charges" placed upon us due to our *aveiros* over the course of the year. This is the day of Yom Kippur, the day when Hashem cleans our slate.

Then comes Succos, when we live and sleep in Hashem's home — the sukkah — never wanting to leave His side again.

This is an example of how the Jewish months and holidays are all interwoven. Our job is to appreciate the wonderful *mo'adim* that Hashem has given us and utilize them to the fullest. May we all grow closer to Hashem by climbing the ladder of *aliyah* throughout the year.

SELICHOS

TUNNEL VISION

Sefer Tehillim describes two very bleak situations.[317] The first one is a totally shattered and poor man who exhausts all avenues of earning a livelihood, to the point where he, his wife, and his thirteen children are left penniless and starving with no one to turn to. He is, as *sefer Tehillim* calls it, completely engulfed — *me'utaf* — in his anguish.

The second scenario is a group of travelers that is searching aimlessly for civilization after being lost in the desert for days. The sand has covered over their footprints, their provisions have run dry, and their hunger and thirst are excruciating. They are completely stranded, boxed in — *me'utaf* — by despair, without any hope of rescue.

Although their quandaries have darkened their world, that darkness actually sets the stage for their salvation. The Maharal writes that when a person places his trust solely in Hashem, Hashem will be there for him, and both of these groups merited just that.[318] There was nowhere for them to turn except towards Hashem, and when they turned to Him and poured out their hearts, He was there for them and saved them.

317 *Tehillim* 102 and 107. The scenarios are embellished here.

318 Maharal, *Be'er HaGolah*, the fourth *be'er*, pg. 74, s.v. *"Perek kama d'Rosh Hashanah."*

The Maharal connects the word *me'utaf*, which was used by *sefer Tehillim* to describe these two scenarios, to a Gemara that uses the same word to teach us how to recite Hashem's Thirteen Attributes of Mercy.

The Gemara relates that Hashem told Moshe that whenever Klal Yisroel sins, they should first wrap themselves — *me'utaf* — in a *tallis* and then recite the Thirteen Attributes of Mercy.[319] The Gemara does not mean that the mere action of wrapping oneself in a *tallis* generates forgiveness. Rather, it has a much deeper meaning.

On a simple level, the Maharal writes that just as a *tallis* hides its wearer from distractions, so too one should take care not to get distracted when saying the Thirteen Attributes of Mercy. We must say them with complete concentration.

On a deeper level, just as a person can only see one thing when he wears a *tallis*, so too we should know that the only thing that can bring forgiveness is Hashem's infinite compassion.

When we ask Hashem for forgiveness for our transgressions and recite the Thirteen Attributes of Mercy, we are obligated to have total reliance in Hashem's infinite compassion and mercy. One should not rely on his mitzvos or good deeds, even together with Hashem's compassion and mercy. Rather, his hope and reliance should be reserved exclusively for Hashem.

If we recognize that the only real channel for forgiveness is Hashem and not our own personal merits, Hashem will be there for us and we will merit true forgiveness.

Just as the poor man and the desert travelers were trapped in their hardships without any hope of salvation except for Hashem, so too we must create for ourselves that feeling, negating the power of any other potential resource of salvation and relying solely on Hashem's mercy. This is the idea of being wrapped up — *me'utaf* — in a *tallis*. Hashem is there for a person as much as the person trusts in and relies on Him. When we do our part and rely solely on Hashem's

319 The Gemara (*Rosh Hashana* 17b) explains the *pasuk*, "*Vayaavor Hashem al panav, va'yikra.*" The Gemara says that Hashem passed in front of Moshe wrapped in a *tallis*.

infinite compassion, then and only then will Hashem grant us a full pardon, as He promised Moshe.

However, if we rely even partially on other things, we will lose the full power of Hashem's infinite compassion. Then we will be forced to generate forgiveness with our own merits, which leaves little room for hope.

We find this idea throughout the *Selichos*: "Neither with kindness nor with good deeds do we come before You. As paupers and as beggars we knock at Your doors, O Compassionate and Gracious One."

May this insight of the Maharal help us appreciate the beauty in the *Selichos* and help us merit a complete forgiveness.[320]

---

320 As we enter into a week of *Selichos*, asking Hashem for forgiveness, we should let the introductory *pasuk* to the *Yud Gimmel Middos*, "*Vayaavor Hashem al panav*," strike a chord. Hashem is reminding us to fulfill our part and have absolute reliance in Him with His attributes of mercy, and then He can forgive us as He promised Moshe.

ROSH HASHANAH

A GOOD AND SWEET YEAR

The widespread custom on Rosh Hashanah is to dip an apple into honey and ask Hashem to bless us with a good and sweet year. However, isn't a sweet year included in a good year? What is a sweet year coming to add?

Although everything that Hashem does is good, not everything that is good is sweet. A person can be blessed with a good year, but not be able to see the goodness. By adding the word sweet to our *tefillah*, we are asking that we should see and feel that goodness as well.

ROSH HASHANAH

THE KING'S PALACE

On Rosh Hashanah, R. Nosson Vochtfogel would remind his *talmidim* of the wonderful opportunities that lie within Rosh Hashanah. He managed to transform a seemingly hard and dry two days of Rosh Hashanah into an extremely powerful and spiritual experience so great that it would change their lives.[321]

"Have you ever forgotten about yourself, even for a moment?" R. Nosson would ask his *talmidim*. "The whole year we are worried about ourselves, our image, our livelihood, our health, our children, our homes, our cars, and even our *Olam Haba*. Rosh Hashanah is a time to switch gears.

"On Rosh Hashanah, we enter into the King's palace. Stop, look around, and absorb all that you can from these two very special days of Rosh Hashanah. Leave your past, present, and future, along with what is important and precious to you outside the palace, and focus on the King's palace and what it represents.

"Open your eyes, my dear *talmidim*, while you are inside and you will find yourself in an entirely different place. A place where Hashem's kingdom matters. A place where goodness and truth shine brightly, and evil and falsehood do not exist. Just listen to the words that we

321 Based on *Leket Ra'shimos, Elul and Yomim Noraim*, pgs. 65–70.

utter in our *tefillos*: 'Hashem should rule over the whole entire world' and 'Every creature should know that Hashem created him.'"

If we follow R. Nosson's directions and live for two whole days in a world of Godliness, a world of Hashem's kingdom and *malchus Shamayim*, chances are that we too, along with our priorities, will change. We could walk out of Rosh Hashanah a new person, perhaps even a *tzaddik*. It is truly a day when we can become different people.

ROSH HASHANAH

SETTING UP THE NEW YEAR

On the surface, every year more or less looks like the next. They all have the same Rosh Hashanah, Chanukah, Succos, Shavous, and Pesach. However, if we look a little bit deeper, we will find that no year resembles the next. The Maharal writes that the Hebrew word for year — *shanah* — comes from the word *shinui*, which means "different," because every year is completely different and unique with its own role.[322]

The reason for that is because every year has its specific task in bringing the world to its completion, as if there are six thousand puzzle pieces corresponding to the world's six thousand years of existence and every one adds it uniqueness to the big picture. The year's task is to fill the world with *kavod Shamayim*.

In order to prepare the upcoming year with the tools needed to facilitate its task, Hashem makes a grand reckoning. He looks at what things added in bringing the *kavod Shamayim* of last year and what could aid the upcoming year as well, and then He rearranges them accordingly.

Perhaps we can liken Rosh Hashanah to a person whose home is undergoing major renovations. He has to decide which pieces of fur-

322 Based on *Sifsei Chaim, Moadim*, vol. 1, pgs. 89–97.

niture, which lights, and which appliances he wants to keep for his new home, and what he needs to get rid of and buy new. So too, on Rosh Hashanah, Hashem is deciding who and what will bring about the *kavod Shamayim* needed in the upcoming year.

This is one of the reasons why all of our *tefillos* on Rosh Hashanah are *tefillos* for *malchus Shamayim*. As we crown Hashem as King, we are expressing our concerns and interests for *kavod Shamayim*. Even if we did not score so high on the *kiddush Hashem* scale in the previous year, Hashem could still decide to keep us alive in light of our concern and interests. We hope that such concern can bring us merits for the upcoming year.

This is why angels, animals, and even inanimate objects are judged on Rosh Hashanah. Although they cannot be held accountable for their action because they do not have free will, nonetheless they still need to be judged to see if they are needed for the *kavod Shamayim* of the upcoming year.

A good year, life, and *parnasah* are some of the tools that Hashem will parcel out in order to facilitate the revelation of *kavod Shamayim* needed this year. This will be given out to the people who really want *kavod Shamayim*. It comes out that Rosh Hashanah is a day to express our concern for *kavod Shamayim* and Hashem's kingdom and to show our loyalty towards it.

May we merit a year of goodness and *brachah*.

YOM KIPPUR

AN OCEAN OF MERCY

Joey had committed a capital offense and was now being charged with the death sentence. Although he felt tremendous remorse, the situation looked hopeless, as no lawyer would come to his defense. His family had organized *Tehillim* rallies and people gave *tzedakah* in his merit, hoping for a miracle before the final verdict.

On the day of the verdict, the judge discharged Joey without any explanation! "Joey, you are free to go."

The prosecuting attorneys were dumbfounded. "But what about..." "How can you ignore..." "Where is the justice?" they shouted. Despite their cries, they could do nothing, and Joey went home a free man.

If we could see what is happening in the spiritual spheres between Rosh Hashanah and Yom Kippur, we might witness something similar to the aforementioned analogy.

We are all on trial on Rosh Hashanah, most probably guilty and empty-handed, without an optimistic outcome. Chances are there is a surplus of prosecuting attorneys against us, and their claims are quite convincing. Yom Kippur is the day when we will hear the final verdict. Hashem, *kaveyachol*, will walk into the courtroom and announce, "Klal Yisroel, I forgive you! You are free to go." All the prosecuting attorneys will be silenced, and the case will be closed.[323]

R. Yechezkel Levenstein describes Yom Kippur as an ocean of mercy. Picture yourself swimming in the middle of the Atlantic Ocean. There are six miles of water underneath you and five thousand miles of water in every direction. Now, turn that water into Hashem's infinite compassion and mercy — an ocean of mercy. That is Yom Kippur, the day when Hashem shows His ultimate dominion and power as He overwrites all the thousands of claims against us and decides to give us life. That is power and compassion in its fullest form.

In addition to Hashem's compassionate ruling, He also removes our *aveiros* and the steel barrier that they have formed between Him and us. Chazal tell us that only Hashem has the power to do this, as He personally comes to clean His children from their dirt, like a mother changing her baby's diaper.[324]

To have the barriers removed is a tremendous gift, and to have our Father in Heaven come clean us on top of that is something that can fill a person's heart with joy for many years to come. This is truly the happiest day of the year for the Jewish people.

Imagine Joey and his family's joy when they heard that he had been acquitted. Now imagine the joy and happiness they will feel when they are reunited. This is Yom Kippur. We have been on trial for forty days, awaiting our verdict, and today we hear the words, "Klal Yisroel, you are free to go. I forgive you." The barriers between Hashem and us have been removed, and we can once again reconnect.

323 This is what Chazal call *hanhagas haYichud*, where Hashem takes total control. The Medrash *Bereishis Rabbah* 3:8 says that Hashem saved one day for Himself, and that day is Yom Kippur. See *Sifsei Chaim*, *Moadim*, vol. 1, pg. 282.

324 Look in *Tomar Devorah*, ch. 1, the third *middah*.

SUCCOS

IF MY ESROG COULD TALK...

As Moishy gazed at his *arba minim* during *Hallel*, he noticed that his *aravos* were crying.

"What is wrong, my dear *aravos*?" Moishy asked in concern.

"We are sad because the *hadassim* have such a beautiful smell and we don't have a smell at all. Why didn't Hashem make us like the beautiful-smelling *hadassim*?"

Now Moishy looked at the *hadassim*. He couldn't believe his eyes, but they were also sad. "What is wrong, my dear *hadassim*?" he asked.

"It isn't fair. Why did Hashem make the *lulav*'s leaves so nice and tall and our leaves so little and round? We want to be the tallest."

The *lulav* wanted to be the *esrog*, and, believe it or not, the *esrog* felt lonely. "It makes me so sad to see everybody else having fun without me," cried the *esrog*. "Why am I always the one that has to be left out?"

Moishy turned to his *arba minim* and told them that they had it all wrong. "Don't you know that Hashem picked you from all the thousands of trees and bushes in the world?

"*Hadassim*, your leaves were picked because of their shape; they resemble a person's eye. And Hashem picked you, *esrog*, because you represent the *tzaddikim*, who have to be separated from the *klal* at times.

"My wonderful *arba minim*, don't be sad because you are not somebody else; be happy because of who you are. Hashem made every single one of you special and unique, and it is because of your uniqueness that you were chosen to be part of the *arba minim*."

How often do we find ourselves using other people's measuring sticks? If we hear the words "Yaakov is smarter than I am" or "Yossi has more friends than I do" ringing in our ears, we must remind ourselves that we are not Yaakov or Yossi. We are ourselves and Hashem made us just the way we are supposed to be. Somehow, we borrowed Yaakov and Yossi's measuring stick, and we left ours behind.

Every Jew is special and has something that only he or she can give to the world. Every Jew has his or her personal *kiddush Hashem* that nobody else can ever make. Discover yours and make it beautiful.[325]

---

325 See *Alei Shor*, vol. 1, pgs. 36–38; and *Michtav M'Eliyahu*, vol. 1, pg. 22.

SHEMINI ATZERES

We have reached an end of a special period. If you remember the story of Yankele in the police station and his cry of "Taaatttyyy!" as he leaped into his father's arms,[326] you will remember that this period started with a tremendous bond between us and Hashem. However, just as all good things must come to an end, so too do these great days of *d'veykus*. We can't live in the King's palace the whole year. By tomorrow we will be back to regular life and everything will turn back to business as usual — except for our new bond with Hashem.

Chazal tell us that Hashem has also enjoyed our closeness and is *kaveyachol* having a hard time saying goodbye. He asked us to make a farewell party, the day of Shemini Atzeres, to express how painful it is to separate.[327]

This farewell party is a call of love from Hashem asking us not to forget Him and the new bond that we have just created with Him throughout the year. Just as a mother wants her traveling son not to forget her, Hashem does not want us to forget Him, *chas v'shalom*.

"Please write me letters from time to time and please don't forget

326 See the essay on Elul above.
327 Based on *Darchei Mussar*.

to call," says the mother to her boy. So too Hashem is telling us with this farewell party, *kaveyachol*, "Please don't leave Me. Make sure you keep up our connection by learning Torah every day, doing mitzvos and by *davening*."

It is hard to say goodbye, but at the same time, we hopefully have a new bond with Hashem that will keep us connected to Him throughout the year.

SIMCHAS TORAH

GETTING "A LITTLE" CARRIED AWAY

If we take a step back and take another look at the dancing of Simchas Torah, we will see that it takes place right in the middle of *davening*. While taking out the *Sefer Torah* from the *Aron haKodesh* to read, we get "a little" carried away and start to dance with the Torah instead of reading it. That dancing is actually an expression of a Jew's uncontrollable joy that manages to rise to the surface.

Our joy stems from two things: the fact that we have the Torah, and that Hashem gave it to us.

To receive a lavish gift can make a person's heart sing, but to receive a lavish gift from a great and esteemed individual is even more reason to be ecstatic. We, the Jewish people, have both. The best gift in the world from the best Giver in the world, and that is the reason for our joy.

R. Simcha Ziskind Brody writes that the *chag* of Shavuos is really the time to appreciate Hashem's gift to us, and that Simchas Torah is the time to appreciate the Giver of that gift, Hashem. We are blessed to have a relationship with Him and to constantly receive His love.[328]

Imagine the Queen of England personally gave you a gift. Even if it was an extremely modest gift, you would still find joy knowing that the Queen gave it to you. You might even boast about it to your friends, saying, "Look at what the Queen of England gave me!"

All the more so for us: knowing that Hashem, the Master of the Universe, gave us something as precious as the Torah, which the Medrash calls "Hashem's only daughter," is definitely cause for celebration.

One of the reasons why Simchas Torah was established at the end of Tishrei was because it needed to come after a month of *d'veykus*. After a month of *teshuvah*, a Rosh Hashanah together with the spiritual cleansing of Yom Kippur, and the living within Hashem's embrace during the whole Succos,[329] we can really begin to feel how fortunate it is to be a Jew. That feeling brings us to such uncontrollable joy that we start to dance with the Torah even in the middle of a *davening*.

---

328 Look in *Saam Derech, Parshas Emor*, pg. 161.

329 The minimum walls for a kosher *succah* are two and a little bit. The Arizal writes it is as if Hashem is giving us a hug with the *succah*. His upper arm is one wall, His forearm is the second wall, and Hashem's hand is the little bit. All together it is like a hug from Hashem.

CHANUKAH

DID YOU EVER GIVE HASHEM A DOZEN ROSES?

R. Yaakov Neiman finds part of the text of *Al HaNissim* rather puzzling. *"Amadeta la'hem ba'eis tzara*sam, *ravta es rivam...* — You [Hashem] stood up for them [Klal Yisroel] in the time of their distress; You took up their grievance, judged their claim, and avenged their wrong." Why was only Klal Yisroel distressed and aggrieved over the calamities that were occurring and not Hashem? After all, the Greeks' objective was to disregard Hashem's Torah and mitzvos. Wouldn't it seem in order to attribute such distress and grievance to Hashem as well?[330]

Secondly, he asks, when we mention Hashem's mercy in the *Al HaNissim*, why do we stress Hashem's abundant mercy — "And You with Your abundant mercy"?[331] Why did we need Hashem's abundant mercy? Why couldn't the usual mercy that sustains the whole world suffice?

The answer that he gives is a fundamental and astonishing one. When Hashem gave us the Torah, He did not give it to us so that He should have servants serving Him, since Hashem does not need

330 Based on *Darchei Mussar*, Chanukah.
331 *"Ve'Atah b'rachamecha harabim."*

us or our favors. He was King before the world was created and will continue to reign even after it is gone. Rather, He gave us His Torah for *our* sake — not His. The Torah is nothing less than oxygen to our souls. *Yiddishkeit* makes our lives worth living by bringing us happiness and meaning. The Torah is ours, and it is our job to appreciate and cherish it. Hashem wants us to have it — but only if we want it.

If Klal Yisroel aren't troubled by the potential threat to their *Yiddishkeit*, then it means that it isn't that precious to them. Consequently, Hashem will not come to their aid and will even permit the destruction of the Torah! Hashem gave the Torah to a nation that would cherish and appreciate it. If Klal Yisroel does not want the Torah, then the purpose of Klal Yisroel and the Torah no longer exists, and without that, there is no purpose to the world.

However, when we recognize the beauty in the Torah and show a deep appreciation for it, even if there is a threat of spiritual annihilation on the horizon, Hashem will be there to help us.

Galus Yavan was a time of extreme threat to our Torah and our *Yiddishkeit*. At that time, the Torah was in danger of destruction, and Klal Yisroel wasn't screaming. The Jewish people didn't appreciate and cherish the Torah enough to try and save it. As a result, they put the whole world in jeopardy. Hashem's ordinary mercy would not have sufficed to save the situation; it called for an enormous amount of mercy.

There was only one way to awaken this mercy, and that was by showing Hashem how precious the Torah was to them. This is what the Chashmona'im did. They were the only ones who truly loved and cherished the Torah. By grieving when the Greeks tried to destroy it, they stirred up a tremendous amount of mercy in Hashem and brought about the miracle of Chanukah.

The Medrash tells a story of a nation that presented a crown made of gold, silver, and priceless stones to its king.[332] The king replied, "I am not interested in your riches; all I want are *shoshanim*, roses." The question arises: If the king really wanted *shoshanim*, couldn't he have

---

332 *Medrash Tehillim* 44. I heard this explanation of the Medrash from R. Shimshon Pincus, *zt"l*.

sold the crown and bought them himself? Certainly not, because *shoshanim* are an expression of love and appreciation. When the king was saying, "All I want are *shoshanim,*" he was really saying that all he wanted was reassurance that his nation cherished and appreciated everything that he did for them.

When the Chashmona'im grieved over the destruction of the Torah, that grief contained such a sense of appreciation in it that it was as if they had just given Hashem a dozen roses. This is what ignited Hashem's abundant mercy, causing Him to save the rest of Klal Yisroel as well.

This is why we say on Chanukah that Hashem performed the miracle of Chanukah for the *shoshanim* — the roses.[333] Hashem performed the miracle for those who expressed their love and appreciation of His Torah — the Chashmona'im.

With this, we can now understand the intent of *Al HaNissim*. Hashem, with Your abundant mercy, You stood up and saved all of Klal Yisroel. Although the imminent threat to their *Yiddishkeit* did not distress them, nonetheless Hashem saved them with His abundant mercy because it distressed their leaders, the Chashmona'im. This is also the reason why He avenged their wrong, because it pained them (the Chashmona'im) when their Torah, which they loved, was being destroyed.

Within the last century, we have witnessed many nations trying to destroy *Yiddishkeit*, to remove *Yidden* from Torah, and to tear down yeshivos and *shuls*. People often ask, "Where is Hashem, and how can He let this happen to His Torah?"

R. Neiman explains that when Klal Yisroel relaxes in its observance of Torah and mitzvos and feels that they can live without it, they are in essence showing that they do not find their happiness and life within the Torah anymore. Consequently, Torah and *Yiddishkeit* can be destroyed.

Our job is to love and cherish the Torah and to find happiness within it. If the nations, assimilation, or anything else attempts to

---

333 *Naasah neis la'shoshanim.*

wipe out any part of the Torah, it should be devastating to us. When we witness *chillul Shabbos* or consider that millions of Jews do not know what *Shema Yisroel* is, we should cry out to Hashem in pain, and in that way, cause Hashem to come to our rescue and save us from our agony.

PURIM

THE JOY OF PURIM

Once there was a king who greatly loved his son the prince, but his son neither loved his father nor appreciated all that his father had done for him. Despite his father's attempts, the prince slowly slipped away. His father had no choice but to send him away to a distant island, where he hoped the prince would one day discover how precious he was to his father and return to him.

Although the prince looked forward to his new life, he also felt abandoned and unloved. However, before he could even begin to wonder where his next meal would come from, an elderly man approached him and inquired, "Have you been to this island before? Do you have a place to sleep? Would you like me to show you around?"

The prince accepted the man's invitation, and soon thereafter this elderly man's home became his new haven.

While the prince was on the island, many unexpected events took place. Once, an unknown hunter miraculously saved his life from a ferocious bear that attacked him in the forest. Another time a stranger reprimanded him for associating with the wrong friends. For some reason, he felt protected and safe on the island, almost as if he had a guardian angel watching over him.

One day, the prince began to dance with an uncontrollable joy. The elderly man asked him, "What is all the commotion about?"

The prince exclaimed, "I finally understand why so many strange events have been happening to me. My father has been behind everything; after all, this is his island. I thought we found each other coincidentally, but I now see it was really my father taking care of me. Even the hunter who saved my life and the stranger who reprimanded me must have been hired by my father!"

The prince cried out in joy, "My father, the king, has been with me from the day that I left him! He still loves me! He still loves me!"

Once the prince realized how much his father loved him, he decided to change his ways and give his father the love and respect that he rightfully deserved.

With this *mashal*, we can begin to appreciate the miracle of Purim and see how it affects our lives.[334]

At the time of the Purim miracle, Klal Yisroel had never experienced *hashgachah pratis* within the darkness of *galus*. All the *hashgachah pratis* that they encountered through the ages occurred through open miracles similar to the Splitting of the Sea.

Purim was the first time that Hashem's *hashgachah* was hidden within the confines of nature. Hashem chose to orchestrate the *hashgachah* from behind the scenes, just as the king in the aforementioned analogy did for his son. This taught Klal Yisroel that even when the *hashgachah* is not apparent, that doesn't mean it's not there; rather, it's only masked by nature.

This is one of the reasons we wear masks on Purim — to remind ourselves that Hashem is wearing the mask of nature and He is behind that mask, tending to us like a shepherd tends to his flock and a mother cares for her child.

In *Megillas Eichah*,[335] Hashem is compared to a ferocious bear. As we saw, R. Shimshon Pincus used to explain this with a *mashal*: Yankele was terrified when his father came home dressed in a bear

334 See the Vilna Gaon's explanation on *Esther* 1:2, which is expounded upon in *Lekach Tov*, *Chaim Shel Torah*, vol. 1.

335 *Eichah* 3:10: "*Dov orev hu li, ari ba'mistarim.*"

costume. He screamed in panic and ran to hide. But once his father picked him up and whispered into his ear, "Don't worry, Yankele, it's me, Tatty," he was able to tolerate the ferocious bear.

R. Pincus would relate this *mashal* on Tishah b'Av to remind us that even our *tzaros* are really Hashem in disguise. Perhaps the *mashal* is appropriate to Purim as well. Purim is the whisper, "It's me, Tatty, and everything is fine. I'm taking care of you!"

Purim is at the end of the yearly cycle of *yomim tovim* because it has something to offer that no other *yom tov* can.[336] Every other *yom tov* corresponds to an open miracle,[337] whereas Purim corresponds to a hidden miracle. This added dimension teaches us that there is *hashgachah pratis* also in the darkness of *galus*.

Even if it appears that Hashem has left us, He is really just hiding behind the mask of nature. Just as the king concealed himself behind his servants and as Yankele's father concealed himself in the bear costume, so too Hashem is concealed behind the mask of nature. A Jew can draw strength, tranquility, and perseverance to brave the roughest storms, knowing that Hashem is right by his side.

Purim is a day to reconnect and to realize what a precious relationship we have with Hashem. The more we open our eyes and see how much Hashem cares for us, the more we will cherish our relationship with Him, and the more we will want to return to Him.[338]

---

336 Even though the Jewish calendar year begins with Tishrei and ends with Elul, the calendar year for the *chagim* begins with Pesach and ends with Purim.

337 Pesach with the *Eser Makkos* and *Kerias Yam Suf*, Shavuos with *Maamad Har Sinai*, Succos with the *Ananei HaKavod*, and so on.

338 This in turn will awaken within us the desire to reaccept the Torah, just as the Jews did in the time of Purim: "*Kimu va'kiblu mah she'kimu kvar.*"

PURIM

IT'S ALL ABOUT BEING THERE

My father, *a"h*, was known for his kindness and generosity. He found his joy in bringing joy to others. He tried to make every customer in his store happy — not because he wanted their money, but because he wanted their smile. People would return items well after their warrantees were over and he would replace them free of charge. He would lower the price or throw in some extras without the customer even asking, just to get that smile.

He would travel to downtown Los Angeles weekly to buy his merchandise and take the rabbi's elderly father along with him, just because it made the rabbi and his father happy. Not only that, but he would send back gifts for the rabbi's children. (The rabbi's father was well into his seventies or eighties, but my father loved it.)

I believe his secret lied in his ability to constantly look outside of himself to see what other people needed. He himself did not have any demands, except that other people should smile.

In theory, we all know that we are supposed to be there for our fellow man, but in practice, we find it hard to put ourselves aside and focus on others.

Purim is a yearly reminder to look outside of ourselves and care for others. The mitzvos of the day require us to be there for our brethren.

"Maybe you don't have enough for your Purim *seudah*? Here's a little something — a gift. I didn't ask if you need it, but I'm sure that it will make you feel good." The *seudah* should be eaten with friends, and the mitzvah of *matanos la'evyonim* is about being there for those in need. We give without them even asking.

In *Shoshanas Yaakov*, we say, *"Bir'osam yachad techeiles Mordechai* — [the Jews] saw together the royal blue of Mordechai." That togetherness comes after the giving and caring, and that is what Purim is all about.

Haman told Achashveirosh that there was a non-unified nation amongst his people. Where was the threat in that? Haman wasn't telling Achashveirosh about a threat; rather, he was informing him of a golden opportunity. "Now is your chance to eradicate the Jews. When they lack unity, the window to destroy them is open before you. Grab it while you can."[339]

In truth, it's not so difficult to be there for others. It's just that our default is to focus on ourselves. The mitzvos of Purim remind us of the beauty and joy in caring for others and teach us how giving to others fills the heart of the giver, along with the heart of the recipient, with joy.[340] Our job is to pour that lesson out into the whole year.

The lesson of Purim is not supposed to be put away for the upcoming year together with the costumes and Purim baskets. It's supposed to travel along with us into the rest of the year and into our lives.

Consider the following example: It took a while for Shoshana to get into her Purim costume, and by the time she reached the bus stop, the school bus had already left. Standing at the corner all alone, she began to cry. Her neighbor Mrs. Marcuson saw her and quickly called her mother, who hurried out to walk Shoshana to school.

Mrs. Marcuson didn't have to use her precious time to call Shoshana's mother, but she did so anyway. Her care and concern for Shoshana turned a potentially scarring experience into a beautiful day filled with precious moments with Mommy.

It's all about being there for others.

---

339 See *Sifsei Chaim, Moadim*, vol. 2, pg. 202.

340 See above on *Parshas Vayigash*.

PESACH

MENTCHLICHKEIT

Moshe Rabbeinu's love and concern for Klal Yisroel was something extraordinary. Even when he was living in Pharaoh's palace, he sought out ways to alleviate Klal Yisroel's pain and distress. In fact, the reason he had to leave Mitzrayim altogether was because he had tried to help a fellow Jew. Even when he was far away, his love and concern for his fellow Jews never faded, and he longed for their redemption.

It is therefore difficult to understand Moshe Rabbeinu's startling reply when Hashem told him to return to Mitzrayim in order to save Klal Yisroel. Moshe said that he could not leave Midian until he had asked Yisro for permission to go. "Yisro has opened his home to me and I am like a son to him," he said. "I owe him my life; I cannot go without his consent."[341]

How are we to understand this puzzling reply? With the annihilation of Klal Yisroel imminent, did Moshe really need to request permission of Yisro before he left? Wouldn't that have put Klal Yisroel into further jeopardy? Even more puzzling is the fact that Moshe ignored Hashem's direct command. Surely Hashem wanted Moshe to leave immediately. How could he delay this by waiting for Yisro's permission?

---

341 *Medrash Tanchuma, Shemos* 16.

R. Chaim Friedlander learns from here a fundamental idea when it comes to mitzvos.[342] A person has to make sure not to trample on any of his *middos* in order to fulfill a mitzvah. This means that when a mitzvah comes our way, we must figure out how we can fulfill it without sacrificing any of our *middos* whatsoever.

Moshe understood that although Hashem commanded him to go to Mitzrayim, it should not be at the expense of his *middos*. That is why Moshe was not willing to leave Midian without first asking Yisro's permission. Yes, it is true that Moshe yearned for the *geulah*, but not if it meant sacrificing his *middah* of appreciation, *hakaras hatov*.

Our lives are so busy, with so much hustle and bustle. We must be careful that when we are on our way to do a mitzvah, whether it is going to *daven* or to learn or even to help a friend in need, we do so without ignoring the feelings of our spouses and family members. Doing mitzvos does not allow us to overlook other people's feelings; on the contrary, it demands absolute *mentchlichkeit*.

The days before Pesach are full of stress, but also full of opportunities to perform many mitzvos. It is of utmost importance that we do not fulfill these mitzvos at the expense of our *middos*. We must try and keep them as perfect as possible.

---

342 *Sifsei Chaim, Moadim*, vol. 2, pg. 270.

PESACH

A SPIRITUAL OVERHAUL

Chazal teach us that there are three partners in every newborn baby: the mother, the father, and Hashem.[343] The red of the body comes from the mother, the white of his skin and bones comes from the father, and Hashem provides us with our *neshamos*. On *leil haSeder* we drink red wine and eat white matzah, and the recitation of the Haggadah parallels our *neshamos*.[344]

Chazal teach us that we became a nation on Pesach and that every Pesach thereafter shares this aspect of rebirth.[345]

Taking this parallel a step further, we can say that just as parents tend to be more cautious with their newborn babies during the first few weeks of their life, so is the Torah more "cautious" with us. Parents try to create a sterile environment as well as fortify their babies with the necessary vitamins and minerals needed to become strong and healthy. They shower their babies with the love they need to grow into well-balanced people.

The Torah takes similar precautions on Pesach, the time of our spiritual rebirth. It creates a spiritually "germ-free" environment by

343 *Niddah* 31a.

344 This essay is based on what I heard from R. Shimshon Pincus, *zt"l*.

345 Although we are not actually born on Pesach, the *yom tov* has a spiritual power that contains an aspect of birth, which makes it into a time of rebirth.

telling us to avoid *chametz*, the food that is symbolic of the *middah* of haughtiness. It also provides us with a food — matzah — that will build up our spiritual "immune system." The *Zohar* calls matzah "the bread of *emunah*." Every bite is like an injection of *emunah* directly into our bloodstream, filling us up with the fundamentals that we so desperately need.

Simultaneously, we refresh our *hashkafos* by reciting the Haggadah, which contains within it all the necessary fundamentals that a Jew needs in order to be spiritually healthy.

By discussing the *Eser Makkos* and *Kerias Yam Suf*, we remind ourselves how Hashem runs the entire world. By telling over the story of *Yetzias Mitzrayim*, we remind ourselves of Hashem's love for us, that He will always be there for us. Finally, the Haggadah helps us channel our feelings of gratitude and appreciation towards Hashem, through the recitation of *Hallel* and *Nishmas*.

Although we do not see this rebirth happening on a physical level, it is happening on a spiritual one. This spiritual rebirth has the power within it to refocus and revive us. It is a real spiritual overhaul, and our job is to use it to the fullest by refocusing on what life is all about and where we are headed.

Leil haSeder is there to help us revive the ideas of *emunah* that so desperately need reviving. The goal is to come away from the Seder with the awareness that Hashem has been taking care of us for over three thousand years and that everything in this world is at His disposal. If a person can honestly say, "It is up to Hashem to decide if my business deal will go through or not," he is doing well.

It is no coincidence that Pesach falls out in the spring when the flowers have begun to blossom. Pesach is also called *Chag haAviv* — the Spring Holiday — because it reminds us of the freshness and rejuvenation that these days have to offer.

We must use our Pesach for a spiritual overhaul, and allow it to take us to the next stage of our *avodas Hashem*.

PESACH

BREAKING FREE

It is well-known that our *yomim tovim* are not just a remembrance of historical events that happened many years ago. They actually contain, on a smaller scale, the special *siyata diShmaya* that Klal Yisroel experienced long ago.

Hashem unleashed a spiritual power of freedom at *Yetzias Mitzrayim*, and that power has been incorporated into the framework of time and is available to us every Pesach. It is for this reason that Pesach is termed *Zeman Cheiruseinu*, "The Time of Our Freedom."[346]

How many of us impose upon ourselves self-limitations? How many of us say "we can't" when we really can? The word *Mitzrayim* comes from the word *meitzar*, which means "limitation" or "border." Hashem used that power of freedom to take Klal Yisroel out of Mitzrayim, which was their *meitzar*, limitation.

Today, we can use that same power to distance ourselves from our own limitations. It is a time to break free and finally reach those levels that we have sought to reach.

For example, if a person has difficulty waking up in the morning, on the days of Pesach he can break through this limitation and begin taking control of his morning hours. Just as Hashem helped the

---

346 This essay is based on *Michtav Me'Eliyahu*, vol. 2, pg. 17.

Jewish people leave their confines, He is here during these days to help us break out of ours.

There are those who explain *yachatz* — the breaking of the middle matzah — in light of this concept, as it symbolizes the breaking through of our limitations.

The seventh day of Pesach is when Hashem removed the greatest barrier — the sea. Some have the custom to pour water on the floor on the seventh day of Pesach and to jump over it at midnight. Using the water as a symbol of their biggest obstacle, they see themselves overcoming it, with Hashem's help.

May we all tap into this holy time and utilize it to break though our limitations and reach the heights that we would not be able to reach during the rest of the year.

SEFIRAS HAOMER

The previous Slonimer Rebbe finds the idea of *Sefiras haOmer* hinted to in the *pasuk*: *"Adam u'beheimah toshia Hashem* — Man and animal Hashem will save."[347] This means to say that Hashem will save a person who elevates himself above his base animalistic tendencies into a human being; a real *mentsch*.[348]

The *korban Omer*, which was brought on the second day of Pesach, was a flour offering made from barely kernels, which is an animal food. At the end of the *sefirah* on Shavous, the *shetei halechem* was brought as the offering. The *shetei halechem* was made from wheat, a food fit for human consumption.

When the Jewish people were in Mitzrayim, they were likened to an animal, however once they left and started the days of *sefirah* they managed to elevate themselves to the status of man. These days of *sefirah* for them, and for us, have been established as days of character trait refinement, as days to transform oneself into a better person — a real *mentsch*. Believe it or not, this is a prerequisite in receiving the Torah, because only a real *mentsch* can be a true recipient of the Torah. This is because the Torah is not similar to the other wisdoms of the world. It is not merely a source of knowledge, but rather a holy entity. The Medrash calls the Torah "Hashem's daughter," and that is why it will only really go to those who have refined themselves.

347 *Tehillim* 36:7.

348 In *Nesivos Shalom*, in his essays on *Sefiras haOmer*.

This is the explanation in the *pasuk* we quoted above. A person who utilized the days of *sefirah* to elevate himself from his animalistic side into a *mentsch* will merit Hashem's salvation, the Torah (because the Torah brings real salvation to our lives), because now he is a true candidate to receive Hashem's daughter, the Torah.

The days before Shavous are important and precious. The power that is hidden inside of them gives us the opportunity to refine the animalistic aspects inside ourselves so that we can merit the receiving of the Torah.

The Ramban goes as far to say that the days of *sefirah* are likened to a Chol haMoed between Pesach and Shavous, making Pesach and Shavous one long *chag* of transformation and self-elevation.

May we all utilize these precious days and elevate ourselves into real *mentschen*.

SHAVUOS

THE REAL TREASURE

The Chafetz Chaim relates the following *mashal:*[349]

The people were so delighted with their new king that they felt it appropriate to make an exquisite crown in honor of his first year of sovereignty. It took three months to find the best goldsmith in the world, two months to send him all the gold, silver, and precious jewels needed for the crown, four months for him to make it, and two months for the finished crown to be returned. At long last, the crown was finished and ready to be presented to the king, and the people began to plan a grand parade in the king's honor.

As the group of soldiers bearing the crown traveled to the king's city, they noticed two farmers off in the distance. One soldier said to another, "Hey, let's have some fun with them."

They placed the crown in a bag, walked over to the farmers, and asked them, "Would you like to see something beautiful?"

"Of course," said the farmers.

When the soldiers took the crown out of the bag, it shone so brightly in the sunlight that both farmers were stunned. "Wow! That is be-u-te-ful," they said.

349 Chafetz Chaim, *Sheim Olam*, end of ch. 14.

"I'll tell you what," said the first soldier to the farmers. "I'll trade you this crown for five of your oxen. Are you interested?"

One of the farmers was about to jump at the offer, but his friend stopped him. "Are you crazy? It's a beautiful crown, but how are you going to pay your bills with it? You can wear it all day and put it on your shelf at night, but it won't put food on the table!"

"Thanks anyway," said the farmer to the soldier, "but I need my five oxen to make a living and your crown won't do that for me."

The two soldiers walked away laughing. "You fools! This crown is worth so much that if you had taken it, you would never have had to work another day in your lives!"

Says the Chafetz Chaim, many people appreciate the Torah and its beauty, but they do not see how it is going to help them make a living. "Sure it's nice, but how are a couple of holy books on the shelf going to help me put food on my table?"

The Torah is priceless and brings us all the *brachos* in the world. Shavuos is the time to appreciate the gift. May we be fortunate to truly value it and appreciate its worth.

THE THREE WEEKS

WHAT WE ARE MISSING

My *rebbi* once related that when he was a *bochur*, a non-Jew once approached him during *Sefiras haOmer* and asked rudely, "Hey, Jew, why don't you clean yourself up and shave?"

My *rebbi* replied, "I am mourning for a very dear and great rabbi that has passed away, and I express my mourning by not shaving."

That experience left its mark on my *rebbi* to this day. Now, when he sees unshaved *Yidden* during *sefirah* or the Three Weeks, he reminds himself that we are mourning over the loss of something very precious.

Chazal established the Three Weeks to enable us to relate to the *churban* of the Beis Hamikdash. So many of us are unable to relate to the *churban*, either because we are too busy to focus on it or because the whole concept is way beyond us. However, once Chazal established the period of *bein ha-meitzarim*, with all of its customs of mourning, they turned the period into a framework for living with the loss of the Beis Hamikdash.

It is important to take advantage of this period and try to connect with earlier times. We should ponder what we once had and what the world would look like if we had the Beis Hamikdash, with all of its open miracles, and focus on the words of the *brachos* of *Ve'Lirusha-layim* and *Es Tzemach Dovid* in *Shemoneh Esrei.*

Let us use the Three Weeks as a vehicle to enrich our lives and make us better, both as an individual and as a people. And just as my *rebbi* reminded himself that something very precious is missing, we should do the same and remind ourselves of the precious things that are missing in our lives, the Beis Hamikdash, and the *Shechinah haKedoshah.*

May we all merit to see the Beis Hamikdash in all of its glory.

TISHAH B'AV

WAITING FOR OUR CHASAN TO COME

The *Medrash Eichah* relates a story of a king who promised to shower his bride with priceless jewelry and clothing.[350] He included his promise in their marriage contract and gave the marriage contract to her so that she could safeguard it. As she walked around with the marriage contract, she felt like the happiest person in the world, with a wonderful husband who was a king, no less, and a plethora of gifts that would come along with him.

However, shortly after the marriage, the king disappeared, leaving his queen alone and penniless. She became the laughingstock of the town. Every time her neighbors saw her, they would mock her, saying that her husband had gone off to another land and would never return. The poor queen would cry with no one to comfort her. Yet when she returned home and reminded herself of the marriage contract her husband had given her, with all of its promises, her wails would subside and she was comforted.

This continued for many years, until one day the king finally re-

350 *Medrash Eichah* 3:7.

turned. Everybody was astonished. The neighbors were ashamed of all the torment they had caused the queen, and the king was amazed at his precious wife's forbearance. He asked her, "How were you able to wait for me all these years? How were you able to tolerate all the torment and mockery from your neighbors all by yourself?"

She replied, "Your promises sustained me. Without those promises, I would not have been able to survive."

This is our story, says the Medrash. The world mocks us daily, saying that our God has left us and He will never come back. We, Klal Yisroel, cry and sigh until we read Hashem's promise. He promised to live with us, walk with us, and be part of our daily lives,[351] and we are still waiting for those promises to be fulfilled. Knowing that Hashem will one day come and save us is what keeps us going and gives us comfort in our times of darkness and exile.

When the *geulah* will come, Hashem will ask us, "How were you able to wait for Me all these years, with all the anti-Semitism, pogroms, and mockery?"

We will answer, "If it wasn't for Your promise, we would not have survived their torment. But since we knew You were coming back, we found our hope in Your promise."

The Medrash concludes with the *pasuk* in *Eichah*, "I will remind myself of this, and that will give me the strength to hope for the future."[352] "This" refers to Hashem's promise. This promise is what keeps us going. Knowing that one day Hashem will come to rescue us from this long and dark *galus* is what sustains us throughout all the difficulties that we experience.

R. Moshe Wolfson writes that *emunah* is imprinted in the DNA of every Jew. Just as a spider naturally knows how to spin a web and a beaver naturally knows how to build a dam, a Jew knows how to believe in Hashem. With the Torah reminding us that Hashem will

351 See *Parshas Bechukosai*, 26:9–12.

352 *Eichah* 3:21, *"Zos ashiv al libi, al kein ochil."*

return, together with the belief that we have in our hearts, let us hope towards a bright new future, the *geulah sheleimah*, speedily in our days, *amen*.

Ani maamin b'emunah sheleimah be'vias ha-mashiach. V'af al pi she'yismamei'a, im kol zeh achakeh lo, be'chol yom she'yavo.